HOOP DREAMS

by

Joshua Reaser

The book is a memoir, and therefore fiction. How reliable is my memory? Good question. I just enjoy writing so take everything with the proverbial grain of salt.

This book is dedicated to Casey, Mike, Andy and Jeremy. Thanks for getting in touch with me in New York and reminding me of my roots.

This book is also dedicated to Tex Williams, who got me started on this project when he asked me to write something about basketball at Saint Albans.

Finally, this book is dedicated to Dad, who taught me how to push through the pain.

Table of Contents

"Every country has its own type of criminal. In America, we got the confidence man. Snake oil salesman, grifter. He don't rob you as much as trick you into robbing yourself. See, 'cause in America, people want to believe. They got that dream. And a dreamer, you can fleece."

—*Fargo,* season 4, episode 7

"It is only for a waking man to tell his dreams."

—Senaca

Introduction

This is a rare occasion for you, dear reader, because what you are about to read is most unusual. It is a memoir by somebody who is not famous and never achieved the dreams he pursued. The author (me) is, by all accounts, somebody who has fallen flat on his face over and over, failed time and again, and has had to struggle and reinvent himself to find a place in this world. But one thing I have always done is continue to get back up, dust myself off, and keep going. This trip down basketball memory lane is a path I have often walked in my ruminations but never in writing, until now. Memory, of course, is spotty at best. This book is less of the facts and more of the yarn that I have told. I am sure that some of the things I have written will be easily contradicted, and for that I do not repent. Many things in my life are full of conundrum and contradiction, and I readily admit that my memory changes with time. I believe that you will understand my motives for writing this book upon completion. While I am the subject, I am not what the book is about. In its simplicity, this book is about identity, change, struggling, and learning. I am a learner, a teacher, a philosopher, a student, a reader, and a writer. I am an artist, a thinker, a dreamer, and a worker. In the midst of the madness of life, and all the bad things that are happening, there are good things happening as well. People are learning, making changes for the better, and growing. What I hope, dear reader, is that you get a little dose of inspiration from reading this book and the motivation to keep learning.

Enjoy.

Joshua Reaser

The Fundamentals of Shooting the Basketball

Among all the fundamentals of the game of basketball, Dad's specialty was shooting the ball. Early on, when I was not yet strong enough to shoot the basketball on a ten-foot regulation rim, Dad put up a low hoop in front of our house, on Lee Street, where we lived, in Saint Albans, WV. The rim was low enough to ensure I could shoot the ball with the correct fundamental form: elbow in, bent wrist, spread fingers, guide hand, fingertip control, follow through.

That was Dad—David Reaser. Basketball had played a big role in his life before I had come around. Long before I was born, he'd been a Parade-All American at Saint Albans High School, a standout player at WVU, and he had come remarkably close to landing a contract to play in the NBA, getting drafted in the fifth round by the Golden State Warriors. He worked out with the team in San Francisco as prospect but was the last player cut on the last day of tryouts.

That was in the '60s. When I was born, in 1979, his playing days were history but his knowledge of the game was still fresh in his mind. And he was a good teacher. He was well-versed in the fundamentals of the game and could break down instruction in a simplified manner, and the first thing he taught me was how to correctly shoot the basketball. Early into my elementary school years, Dad had me shooting the basketball with a fundamentally sound technique, on a low goal, ensuring I developed good habits.

"You gotta practice *making* the shot," he would emphasize.

If I would miss a few shots in a row, he would say, "Don't practice missing. Get closer to the basket, make some shots, then step back. Anybody can throw the ball up there. You've gotta shoot the ball, son, not throw it. And you've gotta make the shot if it's gonna count."

"Aim for the front edge of the rim," he would say. "Control the ball with your fingertips, and keep the ball in the alley. Keep your eye on the rim; don't follow the flight of the ball."

The "alley" was the space between two imaginary lines between me and the rim. Think of gutter lanes on each side of a bowling alley—one line extending from one shoulder to the corresponding side of the rim, the other line from the opposite shoulder to its corresponding side of the rim. When I shot the ball, I would use fingertip control and keep the flight of the basketball in the alley.

If I missed to the right or left, he would say, "Outta the alley," and he would check my focus by asking me, "What side did you miss on?"

It was important to pay attention to *how* I missed so I could make the adjustment for the next shot.

5

"Never miss a shot the same way twice," he would say. "Make the adjust."

The education took; I enjoyed it. It felt good to make shots, and making shots earned Dad's approval. Every day I would be out there, shooting the basketball, repeating in my mind the mantra he taught me: "front edge of the rim, fingertips control, ball in the alley."

If I shot the ball flat, he would say, "You gotta shoot over the rainbow." That was the phrase he used to remind me to put arc on the ball. "Spread your fingers, shoot over the rainbow, and aim for the front edge of the rim."

Front edge of the rim, fingertip control, ball in the alley, over the rainbow.

If you do not shoot over the rainbow—with arc—the projection of the ball, after it leaves your fingertips, is flat and you will more than likely shoot a "brick." Shooting a brick is when you miss the shot by the ball hitting the rim in a straight-on kind of way. When you shoot flat, you have less of a chance getting a "shooters' roll."

Shooters' roll is when your shot is off a little to the left or right, or a little short or long, but still goes in, getting the right bounce, maybe rolling around the rim a little before dropping into hoop.

"To get the shooters' roll, you have to shoot with 'touch'," Dad would say. "You have to have a 'shooters' touch'."

You would get the shooters-roll when you shoot with touch. The ball might hit the rim and bounce around a little, roll, but it'd still drop with good touch. Shooting with touch was when you did all these little things right.

"Success comes by doing the little things correctly," he would say.

What you always wanted for your shot, of course, was "string music."

The sound of string music played when you shot the ball perfectly through the hoop, the basketball not touching the rim as it dropped past and through the net, causing the net to make a "swish" sound as the ball went through *nothing but net.*

"You've gotta make these things habit," Dad explained, "if you're gonna to be a good shot."

He would admonish me to not pay any attention to what other kids did. "You'll see 'em throwin' up the ball from distances they're not strong enough to shoot from. They're just havin' fun but they're practicing bad habits. Only shoot the ball from places you're strong enough to do it right, and make the shot."

He would talk about other things of the game—rules, how to dribble, bounce pass, chest pass, etc.—but shooting was where we spent most of the time. It would be just us out there on the small rim. And when he was not around, it would be just me, on that little rim in front of the house, shooting, over and over, again and again, day after day, as hoop dreams began to develop inside my head. No organized five-on-five or team play of any kind, just me, shooting, practicing, learning how to make shots.

Separated

We lived under the guise of separation. While our residence was in Saint Albans, our social existence was restricted to the religious community of Scott Depot Christ Fellowship, a church in Scott Depot, WV. I was the youngest of three kids. It was Dad, Mom (Mary Jo Reaser), my oldest sister, Jaime, and in the middle, Hilary. Our lives revolved around that church. We would go to church twice on Sunday—morning and evening—spending the entire day in between because Mom and Dad sang in the choir, and choir practice was between the morning and evening services. We would spend other weekday evenings there as well, for things like mid-week evening service, prayer meetings, etc. Mom taught high school English at TVCS (Teays Valley Christian School), so my two sisters, Mom, and I rode together to and from the school.

We would get there early and leave late—Mom was always working overtime—because she was a dedicated teacher, only to drive back in the evening for something on the church agenda. Dad worked for the Chamber of Commerce but he was still involved with the church and school. He was loyal to the dictates of the pastor and was involved in the school; he coached the TVCS high school varsity basketball team.

Our educational lives revolved around the church. It had a private Christian school—TVCS. It was kindergarten through the twelfth grade, so my sisters attended the school as well. At that time, TVCS didn't have any athletic facilities and hardly any athletic programs to speak of. There was a high school basketball team, but they had to practice and play "home" games in gyms belonging to other schools. I never played organized basketball with other kids because in my isolated community of my social existence, such opportunities did not exist.

Religious instruction was first and foremost. I can remember my Sunday schoolteacher to this day. His name was Buster Miles. He was a great storyteller. He was formerly in Army—an infantryman and a veteran of the Vietnam War. He would read a passage from the Bible, tie it into soldiering for God, and then get into the best part—stories from the Vietnam War. He would talk about stuff like Judges chapter seven, where God had Gideon use the 300 men that drank water by bringing the water to their mouths so they could pay attention to their surroundings as they drank. The others had all bent down and put their faces in the water to drink, not paying any attention to their environs. "God uses people that pay attention," he would say, "to what's goin' on around 'em. Even when you're thirsty and hungry, you have to pay attention." And then he would go to Proverbs and read, "And put a knife to thy throat, if thou be a man given to appetite." Then he would get back into the jungles of

Vietnam. He talked about how he could not see more than a few feet past where he'd be standing, hacking with a machete in one hand, rifle in the other. He talked about the snakes and the leaches, the mud and the rain, and sometimes he would stop and stare off into the distance, his eyes watering, and a few tears would go down the side of his face.

The social separation from the neighborhood community kept me away from kids my age. On Lee St., I only knew one other kid—Ryan Fox, who was my best friend. He was born with spina bifida. The brand of his wheelchair was "Quickie," and one day I called him Quick, and the nickname stuck. A lot of people who called him Quick never knew where the nickname came from.

Later in life I would learn about the notion of being "separated" from the world, and how religious people have a propensity to get carried away with the idea. Instead of making it a matter of the heart, they turn it into a physical separation and segregate themselves culturally by isolation, rigid rules, dress codes. The idea is to show evidence that they are representing God on earth, demonstrating how all people should be living. It is also a convenient way to hold each other accountable. But at the time it was not something I thought about because it was the life I was born into.

When Hilary got leukemia, the religious façade started to lose footing. According to my memory, it was start of the ending for not just our involvement in the church but also for Mom and Dad's marriage—although it would take a few years to manifest. Hilary's cancer was the starter pistol that put the storm in motion that would scatter my family to the winds. After a long and bitter struggle over two years with cancer and the torturous experimentation of ignorant doctors, Hilary died at the age of seven. After that, nothing would be the same.

The Next Level

The relationship between Dad and me increasingly began to revolve around one thing—basketball. I grew and got stronger, able to shoot the ball correctly on a regulation ten-foot goal. We practiced at the "dead end," a hoop located at the end of Lee Street, up a hill where the street came to an end. The backboard was white-washed plywood framed in the back with two-by-fours, mounded to a thick metal pole sunk deep into the ground, fixed in concrete. The goal was sturdy. Under the rim was a curb with a 90° edge, and if the ball hit that curb, it would dart down the hill. After a shot, you had to be ready with a quick reaction in case the ball hit the corner of that curb, or you would have to chase to ball all the way down the hill.

Dad and I would do a lot of shooting. We took turns shooting hundred consecutive free throws and see who could get the best percentage, which he always did. It did not stop me from trying. Every once in a while, he would make hundred consecutive shots. He was very competitive. Sometimes he would get past fifty or so consecutive makes, miss one, and be so mad that he would want to start over. When it came to shooting, he was a perfectionist. We were spending time, nearly every day that the weather was good, at the dead end, shooting and playing a little one-on-one.

Going into the sixth grade, I told Dad I wanted to play basketball on a real team. Given the TVCS didn't have a team for sixth-graders, Dad spoke to people at Central Elementary, the local public school, and I was given an opportunity to try out for the sixth-grade basketball team. Because my school didn't provide the opportunity, the rules allowed it. It was a very exciting and somewhat scary opportunity. I did not know any of the other kids; I was stepping outside my social cocoon.

But my desire to play the game was bigger than my fear and I went out and made the team. Shooting the ball was what I did best, and what I tried for most often, but it was not so simple to get a shot playing full-court five-on-five. I was uncomfortable and tried too hard. I was awkward. When we started playing games, I would get around a quarter—sometimes more—of playing time each game, coming off the bench. Organized five-on-five was a huge difference from solitary shooting and one-on-one with Dad. With a team, you have to fit with the chemistry, the flow, the movement of the game. It took me some time to get the hang of it. I had to get to know my teammates. They all knew each other and had been going to school together since kindergarten. They had played together for years. But I was adjusting. It was a big step for me, like entering a new world.

In the middle of the season, there was a Christmas tournament, and it was a bid deal in the local community. The games were played in the Saint Albans High School gym, and there was a fairly large number of people in the stands to watch. We had some family visiting for the holidays, and they came to watch *my* game. I was excited, and I wanted to make sure I played well, maybe even score some points. When the game started, I was sitting on the bench, waiting for my name to be called to sub in.

It was a tight, close game, and as the minutes ticked off the clock, I began to get a sick and horrified feeling in my stomach. I was usually in the game by this time. But the minutes ticked off the clock, and my name wasn't called until the last minute of the first half. Coach Holmes had substituted me in, but only because he wanted a quick word with a starter. Before twenty seconds had passed, I was back on the bench, and I never got back in the game.

I was devastated, crushed, humiliated. It took everything in my power to not let my crushed emotions show on my face. I didn't want to go home and face my family. I wanted to disappear. It was the first game I didn't get to play, and afterwards, I was heartbroken and ashamed. After the game, we lined up and shook hands with the other team and headed back to the locker room. I do not remember if we won the game or not. The final score of the game was the last thing on my mind. It was taking everything within me to hold back the tears.

I walked with the team back to the locker room, doing my best to play it off. Before I got there, I felt a firm hand grip my arm and found myself pulled to the side. It was Dad. One look into his eyes told me he knew everything I was feeling. He knew exactly what I was going through.

"Now, listen, son," he said. "You can either quit and pout about not playin', or you can work harder, get better, and make sure that doesn't happen again."

I nodded, hoping the others could not tell how upset I was. Then he put me on the spot and demanded an answer.

"Which is it going to be?" he said.

"I'll work harder," I said.

My answer was instinctual, a gut reaction. Even still, I meant it.

"We'll start tomorrow," he said.

And after that, everything changed. With Dad, I began to take my game to the next level. With this new level came new rules. Dad took on a different persona. Our workouts were intense. If I did not put out maximum hustle on whatever drill Dad was putting me through, he would stop.

"We don't have to do this," he would say. "If you want t' quit then we'll jus' quit and that'll be the end of it. But I'm not gonna waste my time if you're gonna loaf. It's a waste of both our time. You might as well not even play."

But I wanted to play; I wanted to get better. The heartbreak from being benched was the catalyst. The pain from that was worse than the pain in my side from fatigue. A quick remembrance of sitting on that bench motivated me to push myself and pour all the effort I had into the drill. Dad would keep pushing me.

When I lost focus, he called me out. "You're loafing!"

He would say it with disdain, like it was a crime. He told me that everything had to be done with maxim effort and intensity if I was going to get better.

"You've got to *hustle,*" he would say.

And I would hustle—foot fires, defensive slides, defensive running, back to foot fires, push-ups, free throws—rapid fire. Then the Mikan Drill, rebound drills, tipping the ball on the backboard one hundred times with right and left hand. It was as much about developing a competitive attitude as it was learning new skills;

not that he left that out: he taught me low-post and high-post footwork, to move in straight lines, to make V-cuts, how to go into a triple threat from a reverse pivot. He taught me how to move without the ball, how to get opened.

With shooting, Dad brought some new phrases.

"Shoot at the top of your jump," he would say.

Shooting at the top of your jump means you do not release the ball until you are about to come down from your jump.

"Jump like a bull, shoot like a ballerina," he would say.

That means you go up for a shot in hard, ready to take a hit, like a bull, but as soon as you shoot, the mindset changes to ā ballerina.

"Remember to shoot with touch," he would say. "Shooting is the easiest part of the game," meaning you have to be relaxed and loose when you release the ball.

Dad always had a saying or a phrase ready.

"Fifteen minutes of hard work is better than two hours just playing around," he would say, and after fifteen minutes of working out with Dad, you would be exhausted.

He talked about pain.

"You've gotta push through the pain," he said.

When I was in a drill and started feeling the pain from pushing myself, he would say, "The pain is like a wall, and you've got to break through it."

And I found what he said to be true. The initial pain that I felt, I would push myself through it, and then it would slip my mind, and I would find myself playing hard, in a different zone, my mind wrapped up in the drill.

He talked to me about psychological perspectives, like becoming a different person when I crossed the sidelines and stepped onto the basketball court. Dad explained that you can be nice and friendly off the court, but on the court, there's no such thing as friends. Basketball was a serious game. Winning and losing were at stake. You don't get playing time for being nice; you get playing time by doing all the little things right.

Any distractions were to be sidelined, including girls. Dad had a comical way to demonstrate how foolish it was to spend time with some girl when you could be working on your game.

"Now watch this," Dad would say and place the ball on the floor and walk away about ten paces, then look at the ball and talk to it as if it were a person. "Now don't you go anywhere," he said to the basketball, "I'm going to turn my back, and I don't want you to move." Then he would turn his back to the ball, be quiet for a few beats, then turn to look at the ball again. Seeing that the basketball was in the same spot he left it, he looked back at me to say, "You see that? The ball will listen to you. Try telling a girl to stand still while you've got your back to her. A basketball will be faithful." It was a comic relief, but it still had a serious edge to it: *the game comes first.*

Within a few of weeks of our workouts, I was far more competitive in practice. I was, indeed, becoming a different person on the court. The coaches saw the difference as well and my playing time started to increase accordingly, and after a few games, I was the sixth man—the first player to come off the bench. After a couple more games, and near the end of the season, I no longer coming off the bench, I was starting.

My life became centered around basketball. I was working hard every day. Dad and I were not just going to the dead end anymore, now he was taking me to the gym to work out on real basketball courts. That heartbreaking moment on the Central Elementary team, when I did not get to play, ignited something inside of me that became the foundation of my strength and motivation moving forward. It forced me to make a decision about who I want to be as a player. It awaked a competitive ambition within me. I was not there to just play a game and have fun, I was there to compete. I wanted to be on the floor. I wanted the ball. The heartbreak didn't kill me, it made be stronger.

Basketball at TVCS

The summer going into my seventh-grade year was all business. Dad and I worked out consistently. My goal was to play on the high school varsity basketball team as a seventh-grader. I went through a growth spurt; I was getting better. My focus on the game was all-consuming. Basketball was the one steady thing in my life.

Everywhere else, life was falling apart. At home, more often than not, Dad was not around. He quit the Chamber of Commerce and took a teaching position at Dupont Junior High School and coached the junior high basketball team. He quit coaching the TVCS basketball. Jaime had graduated and moved out of the house. More and more, at home, it was only Mom and me.

My parents' marriage was clearly not working out. Their relationship was turning colder by the day. Dad became quiet and distant with Mom, which drove Mom to anger, and sometimes violence. He would come home late, keep to himself, and not say much. Mom would get angry and explode on him, her temper completely lost. But I knew that whatever she purported to be angry about was never the real problem; the real problem was that her marriage was falling apart, and about that, she was in denial. She did not want it to end, but there was nothing she could do about it, so her frustration manifested in fits of wild rage. It would start in a low growl, the anger gaining momentum, then yelling, then hurling any objects within reach in Dad's direction, his passivity goading her on. Sometimes she would just break something, like smash a plate on the floor or against the wall.

She still loved Dad and did not want to accept that he had grown apart from her. But there was nothing she could do about it. The frustration would build up inside her and eventually overflow in rage and aggression. She was a powerful woman. She would yell, hit, smash things, cry, and it would be scary. She brought the fit to a close by fleeing the house in tears, slamming the door, and driving off in the car to screeching tires. She did not want to lose her temper like that, but she just could not help herself.

Dad never fought back. He just took it quietly, passive-aggressively, sometimes saying things like, "It's something how the devil fights," which might have been a good point but not exactly the best time for such an observation. Such phrases were like throwing gasoline on Mom's anger.

But like Mom, there was not much he could do about the failing marriage either. If you fall out of love, you fall out of love. No one can make a marriage work out that is not meant to work. The marriage was doomed, and Mom pretended not to see it. She wanted the marriage to work so badly. She was so frustrated with how life was turning out. Why was everything so fucked up? How much shit did you have to eat in this lifetime? Exactly how much suffering are you supposed to endure?

I could somewhat understand, and I sympathized with both my parents. I kept it inside. I didn't even talk to Jaime about it. She was long gone and had no idea about what was happening at home. Mom's fits of rage had become a commonplace. After the explosion, she would speed off; Dad and I would clean up, not saying much. We would just fix everything up. Mom did not realize that her explosions were giving him the justification he wanted to actually walk out. Moving out was not any small matter for a man that was, not so long ago, extremely religious and considered divorce a sin against God. After two or three hours, Mom would come back, sorry, apologetic with tears and sincerity, and we would go on as if nothing had happened.

That Dad would leave was not a question of *if*, it was a question of *when*.

One day, Dad had asked me if I would go with him if he moved out. I lied and told him I would, but of course, I would not. After that I was just waiting for the day, wishing he would get it over with. Then the moment arrived and in the midst of one of Mom's outbursts, Dad said he was leaving. There was an awkward moment when he paused in the doorway, expecting me to go with him. But there was no way I could have left Mom like that. He had fallen out of love with her, not me. For me, it was never a question. There was nothing to consider. Mom was seriously struggling, and I knew that hard times would be ahead.

Soon after dad left, and Mom realized it was for real, the cloud of anger and rage departed and was replaced with one of depression. A terrifying darkness took her over, and she was plagued with deep sadness. Dad wanted a divorce, and even though divorce is a common thing, Mom could not accept it. She continued to think Dad would come back. Her depression was total. Years later, after she somewhat recovered (she would never fully recover), she told me that the divorce broke her spirit more than the death of Hilary. At home, she would be in her room, weeping and wailing in the darkness. It is impossible to describe what it was like to hear a human spirit so broken. She would cry, "Oh God," over and over, weeping until she passed out. She could not be consoled. I would just sit there as the sound of agony penetrated my soul. I learned it well and became familiarized with its darkness. I did my best to console Mom, who was beyond suicidal.

I cannot truly say how I felt about this new life. Oliver Stone, in his book *Chasing the Light,* wrote of being a child of divorce, saying that "our lives, our being itself, is the creation of many lies. If my parents had truly known each other before they were married, they would never have united, and I would never have existed. Children like me are born out of that original lie and living a false front; we suffer for it when we feel that nothing can ever be trusted again. Adults become dangerous. Reality becomes loneliness. Love either does not exist or cannot survive. And my past... was a 'fake past'—a delusion." I think that approaches the feeling, but the essence of what I was exposed to, with respect to Mom's depression, is too dark for words. When simply existing becomes torture, you are truly in an abyss devoid of reason and comprehension. There's nothing to say or think about. There are only two choices: kill yourself or endure it. If Mom would have killed herself, I would have understood. Nobody should suffer like that.

I started doing all the cooking and house chores. She would just lie down and cry. Then, on the morning of school days, she would astonishingly pull herself together to go to work, still teaching at TVCS, and give me a ride to school. It was amazing. She would put on the act for work, and when she got home, she dropped the heavy load of putting on the show and got right back to crying. That was my home life from the seventh to the ninth grade. Then she lost her job.

Dad and I had a relationship beyond father and son with basketball. He was my trainer, and I needed basketball more than ever. Basketball was my distraction, my way out of this mess. So, I did not talk to him seriously about Mom. There was nothing to say. There was not anything he could do about it. We continued to meet for workouts. On Saturday, he would take me to Dupont junior high to workout with his team. He had very good players on some of those teams. Two of them would become well-known professional athletes: Jason Williams—who had a career in the NBA—and Randy Moss—who had a career in the NFL.

My game continued to improve. As a seventh-grader, I started on the TVCS high school varsity team with four seniors and would sometimes lead the team in scoring. Looking back, I know that lack of competition had as much to do with my success as my skills, but at the time, I did not realize that. TVCS still did not even have a gym, so we practiced and played home games at a gym in Nitro. But I needed my hoop dreams. One day, I would play in the NBA. Mom would be happy, and we would have plenty of money.

I worked hard and pushed myself. Nobody knew about the hell I was living through at home, but TVCS was a small community, so there were whispers. Sometimes it was hard for me to hold it together. My teammates helped, even though they probably did not realize they were. Jason Brannon and Jamie Wood were two seniors on the team when I was a seventh-grader. They looked out for me and included me socially, even though I was so much younger. They had Mom for a teacher and cared for her deeply. She was always a favorite teacher among the students. TVCS was a small community. Jason Brannon had been a friend and classmate with Hilary before the leukemia took her. One time, before a game, I remember feeling down about what Mom was going through and hardly had my mind on the game. Jason walked over to my locker with a marker and wrote, "Reas the Destroyer," and gave me that fiery look, reminding me that it was time to go kick some ass. Sometimes it is just little things like these that help you keep going. I am still friends with Jason to this day. We are brothers through the Marine Corps and cigar afficionados.

Jamie Wood introduced me to the rap group NWA. I would listen to the *Straight Outta Compton* album on cassette tape over and over. Even though the things they rapped about were out of a different world, there was still something in there that I could relate to, and it was therapeutic. Eventually I would become a fan of jazz music, but during this period my life, rap music carried the day.

Perhaps it was good for me that I had the microcosm of TVCS, for I was able to stand out as I would at no other place. By my ninth-grade season at TVCS, I was averaging over thirty ppg. Larry Hawkins was the point guard and my best friend. He lived in Scott Depot and his parents were going through a breakup as well. We took our frustrations out on the basketball court. He looked to get me the ball every time down the court. He was averaging double figures in assists every game, and I was averaging over thirty. We won a lot of games. The hoop dreams were alive in my head. I saw myself as one day playing in the NBA and believed that I could. Larry and I would not just watch, we also studied basketball games on TV.

But it was well known at the time that TVCS could not compete with the public high schools.

Adding the fact that Mom lost her job, the decision was easy. There would be some people that said so what if I scored over thirty a game at TVCS? I was not playing against public schools. It was not like how it is in New York City, where the private schools are often the better schools. I had to transfer to St. Albans, if not for anything else, to prove my skills against the "best competition."

That I thought of the competition in Kanawha County, WV, as the best competition shows how deluded I was about how good players were in the national context. It would take a few more years to realize where I stood compared to the real, not national, competition. But at the time, I was living my hoop dreams. And God knows I needed them because the one thing Mom got herself together for was gone. Mom felt she was being rejected from the Scott Depot community. She believed she was losing her job because there were rules against divorce. Then she injured her knee in a freak accident, and while getting that checkout, she found out she had breast cancer. If it was not one thing, it was another. She was getting a serious beatdown from life. No mercy, UFC style. Just knocked down and dragged through the mud. That she continued to have faith in God is quite a testimony. She began to realize the church was more cultish than spiritual and that many aspects of religion were about control, not about faith, and she continued to believe in God; that all of this would somehow work out. I would still sometimes find her praying or leafing through the Bible.

Tex Williams and the Saint Albans Red Dragons

Playing for Coach Tex Williams was a big change. To go along with his intense coaching style was an intense look: fiery eyes and pronounced jaw, arms so long they seemed to hang past his knees, a slight bend at the elbow as if he were ready to draw pistols from imaginary side holsters. His typical getup was basketball sneakers, polo shirt snuggly tucked into tracksuit pants high on the waist, whistle around the neck, and his plans written out on paper that would be rolled up and in the grip of his hand. When I would come to practice early, he was often behind the scorer's table, writing, scribbling down plans for practice, drawing up plays.

Coach Tex Williams was very professional. He had a passion for the game of basketball that was not limited to the regular season: it was year 'round. He organized open gyms, summer league tournaments—indoor and outdoor—and attracted current and former college ballplayers to compete. In the summer, he held basketball camps, which I had attended before I came to Saint Albans High School as a player.

His dedication to the game was self-evident. Coach Williams was not just a coach, Tex was an organizer, a promotor, and an administrator. He created opportunities for players to play. He could turn a regular tournament into something bigger, like having it moved from the local gym to the Civic Center, generating a stir about it in the newspapers and causing more people to get involved along the way. He cared about the community and put out a great deal of time and energy, using the game of basketball—a vehicle to engage a number of countless people in a positive way.

Coach Tex Williams was not just a coach, he was a student of the contemporary, fast-evolving game of basketball, and he adapted his coaching style to the way the game was changing. This is what really set Tex apart from the other coaches I had known and played for, and it highlighted a problem with my game. I would need to change my style and develop a different set of skills if I were ever going to be recruited to play Division I basketball.

Tex was the first coach to inform me that I had a problem with my game: I was playing out of position. With my size and build, I needed to play a guard, the perimeter, be a back-court player. I *could* play the post at Saint Albans and score a lot of points, but that would not help me get in the big-time college game. Scoring thirty in the post would not get me recruited.

I was probably around 6'3" as a sophomore, maybe already 6'4". As a senior, I'd be 6'5" and that would be as tall as I would ever get. My growth spurts were early in life. Compared to everybody around me, in the small community of

Scott Depot and St. Albans, it was easy to believe that I was tall because in comparison to others, I was. I was always one of the tallest guys on the team, if not the tallest. And pivot play was Dad's area of expertise; it was the position he trained me to play. I didn't realize it yet, but compared to good post players outside of my home community, among those recruited to play mid-major to major Division I basketball, I had the build for a short and slim back-court player.

But I did not have the experience playing against these players to comprehend this. On top of that, I was very successful in comparison to my peers. I did not grasp the gravity of Coach William's warning. I was a big fish in my small pond. I had not seen the fish in the rivers and oceans beyond. Tex had seen, and so he pushed me to improve my guard skills. I did not comprehend this at the time, but I had been trained to develop a style of game that was on the losing side of a kind of culture war as typified by the difference between the NBA and the ABA. Success in the modern game of basketball demanded certain elements of style that Dad actually discouraged and saw as bad basketball.

The game had been rapidly changing. 1996 was the year of "The Untouchables." Kentucky had a 32–2 record and won the NCAA Championship with Coach Rick Pitino. They were a team that did not run strict offensive sets for catch-and-shoot openings, nor was getting the ball to the post a mandatory first option. These players were not just *allowed*, they were *expected* to create their own shot and shoot off the dribble.

My ball-handling skills were suspect. I rarely worked on them. I hardly ever worked on creating my own shot or scoring off the dribble. I was trained to move without the ball and get opened in a disciplined offence where the ball would be put into my hands. I had basically been given special treatment at TVCS.

But even at the Saint Albans, I was "big" in comparison to my peers, and I was automatic in scoring in the post, so I was always looking to post up. Coach Williams pushed me to play more in the backcourt, which was remarkable because most coaches would have been more concerned with just winning the next game and keeping me in the post where I was far better at scoring, with my back to the basket. Coach Williams had more of a long-term vision and a better understanding of what kind of players the college recruiting market was on the lookout for.

Dad did not like the way the game was changing, and I think he would be the first to admit this, even today. To him, it did not matter that Kentucky won the championship. They were a run-and-gun team and it was not good basketball. *Period.* It was a selfish play. And you could not really argue with him because he would pull rank with his experience. After all, he was a Parade All-American in high school; he was an all-time leading scorer at WVU; he was drafted to the NBA. *He knew better.* Kentucky was a run-and-gun team that shot too many three-pointers and did not get the ball to the post. The way Kentucky played the game—*and was being played all over the nation*—was rewarding selfishness, he thought. Players were taking bad shots. Too much "hot-dogging," he would say.

And you could not really blame him. The game started changing at a mind-bending pace in the '80s. The NCAA didn't universally implement the three-point line until 1986, high school basketball following suit a year later, in 1987. To put things into perspective, when I began my sophomore year at Saint Albans High School, the three-point line had only been a fixture of the high school game for *nine years*. The three-point line, in combination with the shot clock, had revolutionized the game. This happened *years* after Dad's playing days were over. The game was now demanding a completely different back-court style that would not have been smart in the post three-point line and shot-clock era.

To basketball purists like Dad—and this is just my opinion—the swagger of the late '60s and '70s ABA had, by the '90s, infiltrated the game and was perverting the values the game was supposed to teach: patience, conservatism. But the changes in the rules made these stylistic changes inevitable. The three-point line and shot clock made it, at times, more viable for a player to take a three-point shot off the dribble as opposed to the wait of a good post entry pass.

Michael Jordan's arrival was like the final punctuation mark. Dad would shake his head and struggle to accept it. He would say things like, "Michael Jordan is a great player, but he's bad for the game."

"What do you mean?" I would say.

"Nobody else can play like that," he would say. "Kids are gonna to try to play like him and they can't do it. Jordan is good enough to take those bad shots but nobody else is. They'll see him do it and try to be like him. It's bad for the game."

Dad could not get behind Coach Williams' style of coaching, and I was seeing less and less of him. He had been out of the house for a few years by this time and was only hanging around Saint Albans basketball, most likely, because of me. He had a kind of legendary status as a former All-American at St. Albans and standout at WVU. Coach Williams respected Dad's basketball history and judgment, so he was able to come into our practice any time. Coach Williams was not aware of the things that were happening between with Mom and me at home. I did not volunteer that kind of information. It is only now, after many years, that I am able to think back on those times with this level of reflection.

I had to work out on my own, or with Coach Williams, to improve my guard play. I struggled, and we lost a lot of games. I still scored over twenty ppg for the season, but we did not have a good season. It was a tough adjustment from TVCS, where I could play all day in the post, Larry Hawkins always getting me the ball, scoring at will. Coach Williams expected the leaders on the court to use our judgment and gave us flexibility and room to exercise our creativity and basketball IQ. This was a new challenge for me as a player. I did not have great natural athletic ability. I worked very hard on the skills in which I was proficient. I would spend hours in the gym before and after practice. No one could question my dedication and work ethic, but becoming great at something is not just about working hard; *it's about working smart.* Something I had yet to learn. Elevating your game is not about hard work, but *how smartly you work hard.* I worked harder than any other player, but I often did not work smart on the guard skill that I would need to play college ball.

For my size and ability, I was playing in the past. I did not realize this yet but others did. On January 5, 1996, *Daily Mail* sportswriter Tom Aluise wrote a feature on me in the *Charleston* newspaper, titled "Reaser Stuck in the '50s." It was a positive article, so at the time, I did not see the admonishment and prophetical warning, but it was there—in the headline! In the article, Coach Williams said, "I believe after he gets a few games under his belt and realizes he has to make adjustments to the different things teams throw at him, you'll see a really outstanding player." *I believe after he . . . realizes he has to make adjustments.* It was not a matter of hard work for me—I had the work ethic—it was a matter of changing what I worked on. By the time a player gets to high school, it is difficult to make big adjustments. The longer you do something, the more habit it becomes and the harder it is to change.

And then there was the fact that I was using basketball as a distraction from the horror that was happening at home. It was not exactly as if I had a healthy point of view. I was struggling emotionally and had a lot of bottled-up anger that I did not even understand. My problems at home were far more serious than on the court. Mom was going through hell. She had lost her teaching job at TVCS. She was still resisting divorce. Dad wanted a divorce and was pushing full throttle. I do not know why, but we had to move out of the house. Mom told me that Dad wanted the money so he could buy himself a different house. But Mom was angry, and I did not know what to believe. Either way, we had to move. The crying continued. She was not able to get it together. Dad took a teaching job at St. Albans high school. He was always around the school, so

Mom was terrified of coming around, or to my games. The stress and madness never let up.

As my sophomore year at Saint Albans came to a close, the feeling was that we were going to be homeless soon. Mom still did not have a job. She continued to cry herself to sleep at night. She would still talk about how she wanted the marriage to work out, even as the divorce proceedings were turning ugly. Mom would cry about Dad having a good lawyer and playing hardball. "Why?" she would cry out. "How can this be happening?" she would say to the sky. She stayed depressed. I started turning to alcohol. Few people realized, but I was losing my grip. I did my best to hide it.

I was still clinging to my hoop dreams. At least I had basketball, but I was starting to let my anger get the best of me. My friend Larry Hawkins would come over and we would hatch plans to vandalize the homes and property of the people who were hurting Mom. I had had enough. It was time to hoist up the black flag. Somebody had to fight back for Mom.

Larry and I carried out a few of those plans and landed into some trouble with the law. When the police got involved, Mom seemed to wake up. Between the trouble I was starting and us having to move out of the house, maybe it was time to get away, make a move. I did not know what we were going to do, but I knew we had to do something.

Morgantown

When you cannot move your perspective and your mind is stuck in the gutter, sometimes you have to change your location: go *somewhere*; *anywhere* will do. If you cannot move your thoughts, your feet will have to do. Cicero wrote, "Also sometimes the mind must be diverted to other interests, preoccupations, cares, business; finally, it is often to be cured by a change of place, as with sick people who are slow in convalescing."

Toward the end of my sophomore year, my uncle Will—Mom's youngest brother—moved from Canaan Valley to Morgantown with his family. His oldest son—my cousin, Tyzok—and I were close, Mom was close to Will, and thus was the idea conceived: we would move to Morgantown. It was spontaneous, a leap of faith, and had to be done. Leaving the St. Albans basketball team was the only reservation, the only downer, but with Dad always around—teaching at the school, hanging around practice and games—had shut Mom out. I do not blame him. I know that was not his intention. It was just one of those *life isn't fair* situations. His presence backed her into a dark corner. I always knew that Dad simply loved me and was interested in my progression. As the saying goes: *shit happens*. You learn to deal with it and move on.

Coach Williams and I had often talked about the coming season, looking forward to it. Brett Nelson was coming, bringing the back-court presence we needed. But the *shit happens* issues dominated the landscape. Mental health and peace of mind are foundational, without which you simply cannot live the day-to-day. You take life for granted when the gun is not put to your head, and for those who do not know, depression is one of the most destructive lethal weapons.

As plans developed in regard to the move to Morgantown, Mom started feeling better. There were distractions: things to be done, actions to be made. It had more of a breakout feel, an escape, as opposed to a simple move. We could do this. I was not giving up on my hoop dreams. I would still play. I was confident enough that I could play on any team where I landed. I believe in myself as a basketball player. I would figure it out when we got to Morgantown. I would see about the team once we settled in, and I found out where I would be going to school.

And so, with a modicum of advanced preparation and a little help from friends, Mom and I made the move. That it was the right move was immediately manifested. As we set off on the drive, just as we were leaving Saint Albans, the song *Give Me One Reason* by Tracy Chapman came on the radio.

> Give me one reason to stay here
> And I'll turn right back around
> Give me one reason to stay here

And I'll turn right back around
Said I don't want to leave you lonely
You got to make me change my mind

It was the first time I saw relief flow through Mom. She sang out along with the song as we made our escape. She was still crying but this time the tears had an element of letting go, a hint of release. There is a big difference. No words could express how good it felt to see her come alive like that, showing traces of recovery.

We moved into an apartment on South High St. The pressure of getting started in a new place was the distraction Mom needed. We lived in a small apartment with Ashley—one of Mom's former students that was like family—and my cousin, Tyzok. I enrolled in Morgantown High. Tom Yester was the basketball coach. I contacted him as soon as possible to introduce myself and told him that Mom and I moved to Morgantown and enrolled in Morgantown High School due to some family issues back at St. Albans, where I had played for Coach Tex Williams. I told him I was looking forward to the tryouts, playing with Morgantown.

All seemed copacetic. The school was within walking distance from our apartment, and by the time school started, Mom had gotten two jobs: teaching in a prison during the day and working retail for JCPenney in the evening. But getting those jobs took some time, and a paycheck even longer. We did not have any money. So, we did what we had to do. Tyzok and I would go to the store during a crowded time, fill up the grocery cart, wait for the right time, and then push the full grocery cart through an empty isle and right out the door—confident, smooth—as if we were doing nothing wrong. We were like any other customer. And we did not get caught.

We did not have money to buy any clothes for school, so when Mom got the job at JCPenney, just before school started, I would take clothes to her checkout line, and she would ring up a fraction of the items. We never got caught running that hustle either. But after Mom started getting paychecks, we cut those hustles out. We knew better, knew that stealing was wrong. But when life drops you into a sewer, you do not come out smelling like a rose. You scratch and claw your way out and clean up first chance you get.

Morgantown was a big change. It was a college town, home of WVU. Down the street from our apartment, across a bridge, was High St. It had a nice vibe to it. The kind of energy in the air was a new experience, festive. It seemed to be a fusion of hippie, hip-hop, and academic culture. But there was not nearly as much basketball being played. In Saint Albans, there were always games, if not at a park then at an open gym at *some* high school: St. Albans, Nitro, South Charleston, Capital, or at the colleges—State or UC.

There were two high schools in Morgantown but not many open gyms. Accustomed to a daily workout routine, I looked for an indoor gym to practice. It was not easy to find, but find a place I did. Tyzok and I would break into the old WVU field house—where WVU played home basketball games when Dad played—which was at that time basically abandoned but still had a good court to play on. We would break in through a window, workout, and exit the same way.

When Morgantown High started having open gyms, I made it a point to quickly establish a presence on the court. That I was coming to the team was being spoken of around basketball circles. The newspaper picked up the story: "Team includes transfer Josh Reaser from St. Albans, who should provide added size and strength to the mix," wrote Donna Colebank in the *Dominion Post.* School started and everything was looking good. Coach Yester was similar to Dad in his coaching style, to which my style of play was suited—post play and a disciplined offence to get me the ball.

This would not be so good for helping me adjust my game to become a Division I prospect, but I did not have the experience to really *get it*, and I needed any success I could get at the time. Once again, I was one of the tallest players on the team. What goes for tall in WV high school basketball is not so in the larger basketball world. By late January 1997, I was leading the team in scoring with close to 20 ppg and ten rebounds and we were winning a lot of games. Sportswriter Justin Jackson covered me in an article titled "A Smooth Transition: Reaser, Morgantown a good fit after getting used to each other" in the *Dominion Post.*

The open-court ball handling experience I had gotten from playing for Coach Tex Williams still came in handy every once in a while, even if that meant veering out of Coach Yester's offence. He never liked it when I did that, but sometimes it paid off. In a game against East Fairmont, we were down two points with just five seconds left on the clock. We were inbounding the ball from under the opponent's basket. I demanded the ball from the inbound pass and dribbled the length of the court and nailed a step-back three-pointer as the buzzer was going off. We won the game by one point. We went wild with celebration. The *then* WV Senator Michael A. Oliverio II sent me a congratulatory letter, saying, "As a graduate of MHS, I am always proud to see MHS on the winning side."

Things were going well in Morgantown. We had indeed escaped. Mom seemed to be doing good. Jay-Z's *Reasonable Doubt* was being played everywhere. In the evenings, Ty and I would sometimes get drunk on Colt 45 or Mad Dog 20/20. We had a Golden Retriever named Utah. Life was better. Were it not for my grandmother becoming deathly ill and Tyzok having to leave, we probably never would have left, much less in the middle of the basketball season, and come back to Saint Albans.

Halcyon, my grandmother on Mom's side, became very ill. She was living by herself on McQueen Blvd in Saint Albans, near Saint Albans High School. She did not have much longer to live. Mom needed to move back and help deal with Grandma's last days, the handling and selling of the house on McQueen Blvd, and all the other stuff that comes with the process of a loved one dying. So wanted to. I did not mind going back to play for Coach Williams, so I was cool with whatever Mom needed to do. And so it was that in the middle of the basketball season at Morgantown, we packed up and moved back to Saint Albans.

I told Coach Yester I was sorry about having to leave, but I was not all that sorry. If I was sorry about anything it was that life had to be so hard and disappointing. I was sorry that my sister had to die of cancer, that Mom was struggling, that my family had fallen apart, that life's a bitch and you just have to do what you have got to do. If I was sorry, it was in the abstract. In the novel *Like Lions*, by Brian Panowich, the narrator says, "The saying goes, if something doesn't kill you, it makes you stronger, but the past year had taught Kate better than that. Just because something doesn't kill you, doesn't necessarily mean it makes you anything at all. Sometimes this world can summon up just enough meanness to beat you to the brink of death, but you don't die. You move on, and all you do is recover. That recovery isn't the result of some newly imagined inner strength, it's just that stubborn refusal to feel any more pain. What doesn't kill you, makes you numb, was truer to the point." There was a kind of savagery involved in the simple act of existing. So be it. We were going back to Saint Albans.

I reached out to Coach Tex Williams. He thought we could work everything out and have me back on the team. While Mom put her attention into handling Grandma's affairs, I was getting back into a Red Dragon uniform, where I would finish out my junior and senior year. We moved into my grandmother's house on McQueen Blvd, and just like that, we were back in Saint Albans.

Back at Saint Albans: Junior and Senior Year

I was in good condition, but I still had to get my wind back for the up-tempo game pace Coach Williams had us play. Ever pressing on defense, a regular Coach Williams adage was "playing good defense is the best offence." With Brett Nelson running point, the glove fit perfectly. Nelson could run a team as well as any guard in the state, maybe even the country. He was an offensive threat as soon as he crossed the half-court line. His ability to score as the first option, bringing the ball up the court, forced the defense to pick him up immediately and concentrate their focus on him.

This worked in my favor, as I found myself open for a fast-break layup or open for a spot-up mid-range jump shot. We put up a lot of field goal attempts. I was shooting more attempts as a second option (and second leading scorer behind Nelson), then I was as a first option (and leading scorer) for Morgantown. We pushed the tempo much harder and put up far more shot attempts.

Nelson had established himself as a dominant player. I had never played with someone that could single-handedly talk over a game like he did. I quickly learned to play off his lead. I had never played with a point guard who looked to score, and was so good at it, as Nelson. To put myself in his line of vision, I had to run. And that is what I did. I ran and I hustled up and down the court. I would get on the court and just play as hard as I could.

That fact that I was undersized for my position on the college level was not something I could do much about. I did not yet realize it, but because of my size in relation to the people I grew up with and the way Dad trained me to play, I was in a dead-end role that, while would bring me success in high school, would not get me recruited for the college level. If I were a super talented athlete, perhaps I could have overcome my misplacement. But that was not the case. What I needed was to have spent all those years of working out on back-court fundamentals instead of front-court post play. Now I was at the end of my junior year, coming up on my senior year. I had to make the best of my situation. As they say: *it is what it is*. As I approached my senior year, reality started taking the first steps to invade my hoop dreams. I blocked them out. I had to keep believing.

The basketball court was the one place where I could prove myself. It was a space where I could be *somebody*, and have some success. Off the court was not so easy. Mom was better, but her "better" was still a road to recovery. We still did not have much money and sunk into poverty. Thankfully we were able to get government assistance. The food stamps were a blessing. I would go to Kroger grocery store and get a rotisserie chicken, mac and cheese, soda, and eat well, and get real cash money for change. Mom got a job at a video movie rental store on Kanawha Terrace. Slowly we would paint the rooms and do little things here and there to get Grandma's house ready to sell.

The summer of '97, before my senior season, Coach Williams got me into the Nike All-American basketball camp. That camp would be my first experience playing against peers that were world-class, top-level competition. Players at that camp went on to play big-time college basketball, some skipping college altogether and going to the pros. I played on a team with a player who did just that. His name was Korleone Young. Others, like Corey Maggette, Stromile Swift, Richard Jefferson, Teddy Dupay, and Tayshaun Prince, all went on to play college basketball, many going on to have careers in the NBA. These were the players I went up against and it was when I first saw the actual size of good players who played the position I was playing in WV, up close and personal.

It was an eye-opening experience. It was obvious that I did not have the size or athleticism to hold my own in the post. The coaches just assumed that I was a guard. It was a predicament because I never developed the skill set to compete as a guard on such a high level of play. But Dad had taught me some fundamental skills of the game that could help me get by without being a total disaster: spacing, boxing out, quick-release shooting, moving without the ball, filling the lanes on a fast break. I maximized on these fundamentals and stuck to doing what I could do, existing quietly, like a student who gets a passing grade in class for good behavior as opposed to mastering the content. I might not be a stand out among these players at the Nike Camp, but at least I would not make a fool of myself.

Now I could truly understand what Coach Williams told me as a freshman and why he tried to play me as a guard. I was out of position. Sometimes you have to experience something to learn it. If necessity is the mother of all invention, experience is the mother of all learning. Of course, it is always better to learn from the experience of other people and save yourself the trouble, but sometimes you have the experience yourself. It was not all that bad. The style of play in the games at Nike Camp was the style Coach Williams had his players learn, so while I did not do all that good, I did not do terrible.

I would position myself so as to avoid situations where my weaknesses would be obvious. I moved around the wing, set screens, ran the floor, moved without the ball, kept good spacing, and played fundamentally sound defense. I managed be a factor on the floor while keeping the ball out of my hands. I would never bring the ball up the court or make plays off the dribble. If I caught a pass in motion on the perimeter, and I did not have a catch-and-shoot opportunity, I would use a jab step to back my man up and then hit the next open man with a good pass. *Fake a pass to make a pass.* I did not put the ball on the floor unless it was a clear, one-dripple lane to the basket, and even then, I might take the mid-range jump shot instead, because it was dangerous taking the ball to the basket against players that could seemingly touch the top of the backboard.

The Nike Camp was packed with college recruiters and I would rather have them wonder about my guard skills rather than know the truth. I would show them my work ethic. Hustling and getting back on defense never failed. Some of the guys I would have to guard were better players, so I might knock them to the floor with a hard foul every once in a while.

Moving without the ball is a skill that worked well for me. It is the art of reading what is unfolding on the court, anticipating the moves of your teammates, the defenders, maintaining good floor spacing and getting yourself opened without having the ball. I would move and position myself, making myself available for a pass by anticipating double teams. Not double teams on me but on the good players that were on my team. When my defender would leave me, I would move to be open for a kick-out, putting myself in the line of vision of the player with the ball, and by doing that I would get some passes and knock down a few shots each game. For rebounding, I would always hustle to the weak side whenever a shot went up. If my man did not box me out, and guys were always neglecting to box out, I would snag a few rebounds here and there.

My strategy worked. Even though I was in a major dilemma position wise, I still did fairly well. I started getting recruited by a number of programs, all recruiters that saw me at the Nike Camp. After the camp, I started getting handwritten letters from several Division I programs with regularity: Ohio State, Penn State, Air Force Academy, Radford, Akron, The Citadel, and a few others. Handwritten recruiting letters from college coaches are a way to know if they are seriously considering you. Anybody can get the standard-typed generic letter that goes out to hundreds of players. When a coach is handwriting you a personal note, you know they are seriously considering you for their team.

Back in Saint Albans for my senior year, away from the serious competition of Nike Camp, my out-of-position situation was no longer a problem. High school players that are 6'4" or 6'5", in a small town, are in a tough spot. They are stuck being a "big" player on the team, when in the world of basketball beyond small-town high school, they are small. Because of their situation, they get a false perspective of their potential in the game of basketball and never get a chance to work on the guard skills they will need if they have a chance to play at the next level. In the moment, there was simply nothing I could do about it. My hoop dreams were, more and more, slipping into the realm of faith.

And there was still a reason for the faith. We had a good team. With Chris Knapper, Jason Rader, Brett Nelson, myself, and Casey Quinlan—who would dive into the stands for a loose ball Denis Rodman style—we had high hopes for the season. Nelson ran the show. If our opponent did not stop him, he would come down the court and score. Simple as that. He could handle the ball under pressure, run the point, make plays off the dribble, push the tempo of the game, and force the defense to stop him. This in turn opened me up. With Nelson running the point, I could run the floor, fill the lanes, move without the ball, and play off his lead. We scored a lot of points. When Nelson played his best game, it allowed me to play my best game. Teams could not stop us both. We were probably the best duo in the conference, arguably the state.

The local newspapers would run stories about it: "Nelson, Reaser fuel St. Albans' 71–70 victory," (March 1, 1997, the *Charleston Gazette);* "Nelson to Reaser for 2: Dependable duo leads Dragons by SC," (December 20, 1997, the *Charleston Gazette);* "Reaser, Nelson lead St. Albans," (January 20, 1998, the *Charleston Gazette).* Nelson and I combined for an average of over fifty ppg—Nelson in the thirties, myself in the twenties, for the entire season.

We won games, scored a lot of points, and crowds packed the gym to see the Saint Albans Red Dragons play. There would be standing room only for our home games. The lights would go out and we would take the floor by spotlight, running through fog, *Welcome to the Jungle* blasting from big speakers throughout the gym, Jason Rader always getting everybody hyped.

Coach Williams demanded we play our game and be creative on offence. We always looked to push and fast-break. On defense, we pressed and played man-to-man. The way to get in the dog house with Coach Williams was to loaf and play poor on defense. One thing Coach Williams would not tolerate was loafing on defense. If your man had the ball, you had to be on him, hawking him, digging, talking. If your man did not have the ball, you had better be in the right position, pistols out—one finger on your man, the other toward the ball—off and in-line, ready to help or get back to your defensive assignment.

"Never follow your man," Coach Williams would say of playing defense. "You've gotta lead 'im. When your man makes a cut, he better run into your elbow."

When somebody shot the ball, everybody had to yell "shot!" and before the ball hit the rim, everybody had to be boxing out their man.

"Hit 'em good after the shot goes up, on the boxout," Coach Williams would say about the players that did not take the shot. "The refs always watch the flight of ball after it's shot, so that's the time to get in a quick one." Meaning, give your man a strong elbow, let them feel your presence. Even if you were hot offensively, knocking down shots, Coach Williams would sit you on the bench for sandbagging on defense. Everybody had to play hard and smart on defense.

Were it not for Nelson's foul trouble in the state tournament, the state championship would have been ours. We had the best team in the state. But the refs knew how to stop us: make ridiculous calls on Nelson and put him on the bench with foul trouble. Poor officiating was not just our feeling on the matter; Danny Wells wrote of the game in the *Charleston Gazette* that "the officials took the game away from the players." More than sixty free throws were shot during the game. Our style of play was fast tempo and the officials combated that, keeping the pace of the game slow with their whistles, doing what Martinsburg could never do—stop Brett Nelson.

Deep inside, however, after the game, it was myself I was upset with. I was not able to step up. I had never developed the guard skills I needed to play at the next level. I could not consistently take the inbounds pass and bring the ball up the court and make the plays we needed. I did not have that back-court skills that Coach Williams had pushed me to develop. The last game of the state tournament ended with our freshman guard with the ball in his hands. The opportunity was there for me, but I did not step up. So taking the loss in that way hurt. I could have done it; I had the potential but never had developed that aspect of my game. I had always worked hard but not always smart. I could not have filled Nelson's shoes, but I should have been able to step up and control the game. That is what I would have to be able to do if I was going to play Division I, which I desperately wanted. Unfortunately, while my skills were great for a solid high school career in WV, they were not enough to win the state tournament, nor would they sit well in the eyes of college recruiters.

Despite my good senior year, all the Division I schools that were recruiting me at the beginning of the season—after the Nike Camp—had backed off by the end of the season. In the end, not one Division I school was offering me a scholarship. *Not one*. I only had one full-scholarship offer. It was from UC, University of Charleston, a Division II school nearby Saint Albans, in Charleston.

UC was a good school, and their coach was fervently recruiting me, but I did not want to go to college in the Charleston area for personal reasons, unrelated to basketball. My home situation had worn me down, and the time for a geographic change had come again. Grandma had passed by then, and the house was sold. There would not be much money from the sale because the money would be divided between Mom and her three brothers.

Mom was moving to Manhattan to live with her older brother Jim and his son Phil. Jim was nicknamed "Bread" because where he lived was like a breadbox—always a tiny space maximized to the fullest. Also, he was a nutritionist, so there was a "daily bread" element to his nickname as well.

This was not a random move. The breadbox had been a place of escape for Mom and me over the last few years. We had been spending a few weeks out of each summer with Jim and Phil, in the tiny *breadbox* in Manhattan, ever since Dad moved out. It was a one-room studio apartment, but the ceiling was high, so Bread (Jim) built lofts. There were places to sleep above the living room and kitchen space, so we all had space to sleep in the one room, on the sixth floor of the Galaxy, the apartment building across the street from the Natural Museum of History. Spending time in the breadbox was always a period of endurance training for me. My cousin Phil was a professional runner. He was always training. I would rotate long-distance running one day, and jumping rope the next. Then I would take the C train from the Upper West Side down to West 4th Street, where I played basketball for hours in "the cage."

Mom had been teaching from the time she had graduated college until she lost her job at TVCS. She had been a teacher in Virginia, Tennessee, and West Virginia. She had twenty-some years of experience. But she did not have a retirement. She had used that money for something else when she and Dad were married, assuming it was ok, because Dad still had a retirement plan. With the divorce, she was out of a retirement plan. The $200 every two weeks for alimony that she got, after the divorce was finalized, was not nearly enough to live on. So she devised a plan to go to Manhattan and get a teaching job (she did her research and found out that the Department of Education in NYC had a very good retirement plan) while living in the *breadbox.* She would have to start over again.

Toward the end of basketball season, when I realized that none of the out-of-state colleges that were recruiting me were going to offer me a scholarship, I started entertaining the idea of enlisting in the Marine Corps. ROTC was my favorite class during my senior year because of Major Botizan and Master Sergeant Knight. They were good teachers, both former Marines. They were the first people to plant the seed of the idea in my head to enlist in the Marines.

The teachers and counselors at St. Albans could not understand why I would not take the scholarship to UC. It was hard to explain why I could not go. It was a situation that you had to experience to understand. I had to get out of the state; I had to get away; I had to do *something.* Some things in life you just cannot explain. I would enlist in the Marine Corps before I went to UC.

But because of Coach Fletcher Arritt, the choice did not come down to only those two options. Coach Fletcher Arritt was the head postgraduate basketball coach from Fork Union Military Academy, and he came to pay me a visit after my last game of the state tournament. It was a meeting that opened a door to not only one of the best things that ever happened to me, but, I believe, one of the best things that could have *possibly* happened to me.

Coach Fletcher Arritt and FUMA

Coach Fletcher Arritt was the postgraduate basketball coach and a high school biology teacher at FUMA (Fork Union Military Academy). FUMA was a prep school in Fork Union, Virginia. Coach Arritt saw me play my last game, during the state tournament, and wanted me to come to FUMA for a postgraduate year. He liked the level of hustle and intensity I brought to the game. In the newspaper, sportswriter Danny Wells quoted Coach Arritt as saying, "I walked into the state tournament during the St. Albans game, and I liked the way he played."

Coach Arritt would make the trip to the Charleston Civic Center each year to watch the WV high school basketball tournament, looking to recruit a player for his team. He was from Fayetteville WV and carried an endearing feeling for his home state. When he came to visit me, at the house on McQueen Blvd, he said he liked to get at least one "West Virginia guy" on his team each year. In her biography of Coach Arritt, *Body, Mind, Spirit and Basketball,* Bethany Bradsher wrote that Coach Arritt had a "centuries-long tradition of bringing in players from his home state every season." In 1999, that player was me.

Coach Arritt knew I was playing out of position from the beginning.

"You're playing out of position," Coach Arritt said to me on the visit. "You have to play the perimeter if you're going to play anywhere."

In the newspaper article I quoted before, he told Danny Wells, "Reaser will be moved from a forward position near the basket to a perimeter spot at Fork Union. It's not an easy transformation." Coach Arritt put it to me plainly. I would play the perimeter or I would not play at all. He knew why I was not getting recruited by any Division I programs. It was what Coach Tex Williams had pointed that out to me when I was 15. But back then I could shrug it off. Now, at 18 and my high school career over and done with, I had no choice but to face the problem. FUMA, as it turned out, was the perfect place to make the change.

FUMA was a military prep school with a middle school, high school, and PGs (post-graduates). We were not students, we were *cadets*. We lived in barracks. Your barrack was your company: Alpha Company, Bravo Company, Charlie Company, etc. It was all-male. You wore a uniform, shined your shoes, and stood for inspection. You stood in formations, you marched, you belonged to a squad. The squads made up a platoon, which was the floor you lived on. Three platoons made up a company. PGs lived mixed and scattered among the high school cadets in the barracks. Only in the PG sports programs were we separated from the high school cadets.

The PG year was like another year of high school, but the sports were far more competitive. PG competition was akin to junior college. We competed against other PG teams, like Hargrave and Mount Zion. The idea was to improve your game, increase college exposure, all without losing a year of eligibility in the NCAA. It was very competitive. These were teams that could compete with Division III and Division II college programs. Eleven of us signed a full scholarship to a Division I program by the end of the year at FUMA.

We had very good players. I was competing for time against players like Carlos Dixon—who went on to have an excellent career at Virginia Tech and professionally overseas—and Trello Galloway—who played at Georgia St. and also played professionally overseas. In the post we had Jason Parker, who signed at Kentucky, and

Mike Matthews, who signed at Florida state. My first roommate, Ramod Marshall, signed at Dayton, and my second roommate, Thomas Mobley, signed at College of Charleston.

Coach Arritt kept things simple. We ran two offensive sets: one for a zone defense and the other for a man-to-man. Most teams played us man to man, so we would run the one offence— the passing game—which was a four-out/one-in set. We had a structured fast break we looked to run every time down the floor called "Carolina," and if we did not get a shot off the fast-break action we would flow into the passing game. In the passing game, four guys played the perimeter, one played the post. Perimeter players played off each other's movements, passed and cut, set screens, and kept spacing. Defensively we almost always played man and would either pick up full or half court.

At FUMA, I learned the precious value of free time. I would get to the gym when I could and work on my handles: ball handling drills, full-court dribbling drills, finishing each trip down the floor taking a shot off the dribble. I gained confidence; I got better. The writing on the wall had never been so clear. Before the season started, we would scrimmage on selected evenings called "coaches' night" because college coaches from all over the country would come to watch us play. I was put on notice from the first scrimmage. My teammates had the size and athleticism of the players from the Nike All-American camp. On one of the early plays, I jumped up for a defensive rebound, snatching the ball off the backboard as it bounced off the weak side of the rim. I was still in the air, coming down with the rebound, when Mike Matthews—the 6'11" forward that signed with Florida State—snatched the ball out of my grip and in the same motion slam-dunked the ball over my head for a score, knocking me out of the way as if I were not even there. Some people have to be forced into that "sink or swim" alternative before can clearly see the light and do what needs to be done, and this was the position in which I now found myself.

I was not ready to sink, so I learned. It was a hard road but I took it seriously. It is hard to make a change because the longer you play a certain way, the more habit it becomes, and the harder it is to change. Nevertheless, by the end of the season, I developed into a mid- to low-level Division I caliber player. I worked on my handles and perimeter play every day, and little by little, I got better. To be a viable threat on the perimeter, you have to be able to not only knock down the three and drive with both the left and right (that I could do), but execute a number of moves off the dribble: plant and pull up, step-back, crossover-dribble, hesitation, etc., sometimes using a combination of all these things, from twenty-five feet beyond the basket.

Footwork for the perimeter, while having some similarities, was different from the footwork required for high and low post, playing with your back to the basket. The jab step was used differently, and required more patience, buying time as you created space and considered the shifting defense. Coach Arritt was a master of teaching perimeter footwork, and Coach Arritt, like Coach Tex Williams, had adjusted his coaching to the modern game: more three-pointers and the expectation of his players to create scoring opportunities on individual moves made off the dribble as opposed to structured, pre-planned options on an offense set. Coach Arritt made it his business to make sure his players got scholarships, so he was always a student of the college game.

No one placed players into college on scholarship the way Coach Arritt did. The number of his players that signed for Division I scholarships is incredible. "Between 1970 and

2012, Arritt had more than 500 basketball players and . . . more than 200 went on to play Division I basketball and seven played in the NBA," wrote Bethany Bradsher. He was an incredible coach. Those other players still received scholarships to Division II programs. His coaching, combined with the culture of FUMA, combined to impact an individual to astounding proportions, and the transformation I was able to make went beyond basketball. Bradsher wrote, "More impressive by far are the stories of those who say, with no hesitation, that the one year they spent at Fork Union Military Academy was the most significant year of their life, and Fletcher Arritt one of the most influential people they ever encountered."

My sentiments exactly.

I made some serious improvements to my game and got a full scholarship to Stetson University in DeLand, Florida, but I made many other improvements in my life that went beyond the game of basketball. Coach Arritt was not just an excellent teacher in hoops, he was an excellent biology teacher as well. I know because I took his class. I did not want to, but he did not ask; he just told me I was taking his biology class. This was not good for me because I wanted as little as possible to do with academics. I went to school to play basketball. I did not care about the school part. Academics were something I endured so I could play basketball. If my basketball coach was one of my content area teachers, that would be a conflict. I showed my coaches how hard I worked, while with classroom teachers, I did the bare minimum.

But my assumptions were incorrect. His biology class turned out to be surprisingly interesting. Who makes biology interesting? To this day, I can still remember words like sarcodina, ciliophora, and zoomastigina. He was good at explaining things in a way that made it relevant to your life. He could get you to see a thing the way he saw it. He was incredibly smart and had a very smooth, logical way of reasoning. He was not domineering in the least, yet he still commanded an incredible amount of respect. You did not realize it at first, but after a spending enough time with him, you would find yourself really listening to him. He was a wise man in a light, natural kind of way.

It was as if Coach Arritt was born to coach at and teach at FUMA. He could use the rules and culture of the institution to keep out the players that could not, or would not, adapt to the humility and self-discipline it took just to make it through the average FUMA day. A regular day at FUMA packed. Every weekday, for the duration of the day, from sunup to sundown, our schedule was full: reveille, field day, formation, chow, school, chow, school, chapel, break, formation, break, basketball practice, chow, break, field day, study CQ, taps, lights out. Coach considered our following the FUMA rules and adjusting to its culture as important as anything that happened in practice.

At FUMA, Coach Arritt could keep his players from what he called "the five Ps." The absence of the five Ps was absolutely essential for a player to improve his game and get his head together, Coach Arritt would say. The five Ps were *phones, parents, press, posse,* and *perfume.* Bethany Bradsher explains Coach Arritt's philosophy perfectly: "Players were almost never permitted to use cell phones, separated from hovering parents obsessing about their son's playing time, disengaged from much of the media, away from friends who might drag them down and miles away from any young ladies." For a player, of course, the absence of the five Ps was a tough adjustment. We are so influenced by these things and we hardly realize or think about what kind of influence the five Ps has on our lives. It is important to take the time to disconnect from these things to get to know oneself a little better.

Outside of Coach Arritt and basketball, the biggest gamechanger at FUMA for me ended up being the nightly mandatory study time called study CQ, which soon became a time where I would engage myself in a genuinely intellectual way. Prior to FUMA, such a thing was nonexistent in my life.

CQ was shorthand for "Call to Quarters." During CQ, you would sit in your chair, at your desk, in your barracks room, with the door propped opened. You were not allowed to talk, eat, play music, watch television, sleep, or visit other cadets' rooms. Study CQ lasted an hour and a half, and the only thing you could do for the durations was study. It did not matter whether you were finished with your school work or not. There was no such thing as "finished" before study CQ was over. It was over when the hour and a half were complete and the bugle sounded.

If you had completed all your assignments for class then you could go over the material again, read, or write for the remainder of the time. Reading and writing were the only activities where broad freedoms were allowed. It did not matter what you were reading, so long as you were reading, and it did not matter what you were writing, so long as you were writing.

Otherwise, there were no exceptions. CQ was supervised by roaming FUMA staff. If you were caught breaking any of the rules, you would get "stuck" with demerits, and the next morning your name would be on the "stick pad," a list that Coach Arritt checked first thing in the morning every day. He would be looking for the names of his players, and if your name was on that list, you did not suit up when practice rolled around. If it happened to be a game day and your name was on the stick pad, you would not be dressing for the game. No exceptions, even if a college recruiter was coming to watch you play.

Every once in a while, the rule was proved by a player, and Coach Arritt always lived up to his word. So I followed the rules. For the most part, we all did. And, as it were, inadvertently, I picked up two habits that would stick with me beyond basketball: reading and writing for pleasure. Prior to FUMA, I would only sit down to study—in the academic sense—at the last minute, and even then, only when I was in a situation where my basketball eligibility could be in jeopardy because of poor grades. I would never study for the inherent value of studying, like I would for basketball. I never dedicated time to reading or writing for the sake of simply learning or developing my mind and skills in the intellectual game. The only thing I would read was the newspapers, and I would only do that to look for my name in the sports section. And writing, even less. The only time I'd do any writing was for an assignment, and even then, it would be low-quality work with minimum effort.

This would change in study CQ.

At first, sitting at my desk, in the silence, bored out of my mind, I started keeping a kind of journal. Nothing serious or exact in any sense, I would just bullshit along the lines of a composition notebook, usually venting about how ridiculous study CQ was, or something else about this new world of FUMA in which I had found myself trapped. Then I started writing letters to Mom in Manhattan and my sister, Jaime, in Pittsburg. I also had a girlfriend in college and I would write her as well.

Soon after I started writing letters, I got a package in the mail from my sister. It was a pocket dictionary with an accompanying note, in which she informed me that I misspelled too many words. She said I should start looking up the words I was not sure how to spell. I just laughed. At that time in my life, I knew I misspelled a lot of words, but I did not care. I could not have cared less about spelling. *Close enough* was fine with me. As long as I was in the ballpark, anybody could figure out what I was saying. That is just how I felt about it. Learning the trickery of spelling was a fool's game. I considered it ridiculous to include a "silent" letter in a word. The whole idea of having words spelled differently from the way they sounded seemed to me like a dirty joke, a hustle simply to make spelling important, or difficult. I might write psychology, for example, "sicology" or "cykology." It was all the same to me. I did not see the importance. Plus, it was a way to rebel.

But in study CQ, I had nothing better to do, so I started writing draft letters, reading them over, looking for words I had likely misspelled. Then I would look them up, correct them, and rewrite the letter with all the words spelled correctly. Looking up words in a dictionary was as good a way as any to knock off the minutes of study CQ. I would find the word, and then my eyes would drift over and notice if the word was an adjective, adverb, or whatever. Then I would check out the various contexts and definitions of the word. I started thinking about words more deeply, all in a natural, unforced kind of way. Looking back, it seems very ironic that being subjected to the enforcement of such strict rules helped bring forth a new kind of creativity of mind within me. It showed me that it is important to give yourself rules to live by, restrictions to impose on yourself, in order to help you get things done and have some accomplishments in your life. For personal creativity to develop and flourish within the individual, he needs certain governing parameters established and imposed upon himself.

Every night, I would be sitting at my desk, writing, looking up words, thinking about the words I had looked up, and then re-writing. Perhaps it was the wrong word? Maybe there was a better word? I was developing an interest in reading and writing, which would become more important to me as my prospects of playing basketball diminished. There would be times where I would keep writing even when study CQ was over because I was not done. Such a thing was nothing short of a miracle, and I was doing it without even thinking about it. In its mysterious way, basketball had led me to develop interests that would serve me long after I stopped playing, even though I would not realize it for another few years down the road.

FUMA has a motto: body, mind, spirit. When I arrived at FUMA, I was only interested in the body—the sports. By the time I left, I was interested in not just the body but the mind as well. And once you become interested in developing the mind, your spirit follows. From the time I started working out with Dad on my basketball skills to when I arrived at FUMA, my entire identity had been wrapped up in being a great basketball player. But in study CQ, I started to develop a different kind of identity as a reader and a writer. To be sure it was just a start. My academic skills were still way behind and deficient for my age. But I knew how to work hard, and if I were ever to focus my ambitions on learning, reading, and writing, there was no doubt that I would be able to make some serious gains.

Under Coach Arritt and the surrounding culture of FUMA, I was able to mature and grow in many ways with respect to self-discipline, sports, and academics. I had also taken a liking to the military side of the culture. It was not that I enjoyed it, but I enjoyed how much more I was able to accomplish under military structure. It is not a magic pill; it does not work for some people, but it worked for me. Once again, I began to consider enlisting in the Marine Corps, even though I had several scholarship offers to play basketball. I had a good idea that I would not be able to make it to the NBA anyways, so why waste my time? It is not that I thought of college as a waste, but I was not interested in any particular subject, and even though I would not have to pay for tuition, room, board, and all that kind of thing, I would still need money. I was thinking why not just get a career started in the military?

I had been growing up with hoop dreams—of playing bigtime college ball and then on to the NBA. I felt good about the progress I had made at FUMA, but all my scholarships were to low-level Division I teams. Even signing at any of the schools that were offering was still not going to change that reality. What was worse was that I had played against guys that were good enough to play major-level Division I basketball and had the talent to go pros, and I knew that I had nowhere near the athleticism or skills that I would need to make it to any level higher than low-level Division I basketball. I was starting to realize that my hoop dreams were a mirage.

I quietly started making plans to enlist in the Marine Corps. I did not tell Coach Arritt because I knew he would object. He prized education. For him it was less about the basketball and more about getting a college degree. Basketball was a vehicle that you use to pay for college. But I was still immature on that score and did not want to play if I could not see a future in it. Plus, I hated sitting on the bench, and I would rather not play then have to be a bench warmer. I wrote a letter to Mom, who was now a public-school teacher in Harlem, and told her about my plans to enlist in the Marines. A week later, Coach Arritt called me into his office.

"Reaser," said coach Arritt. "What's this enlistin' in the Marine Corps talk I'm hearing?"

How did Coach Arritt know that? "I just never liked school all that much. I was thinkin' college might not be for me."

"Listen here, Reaser," said coach Arritt. "You're gonna go to college. Go on and take that visit to Stetson. Murray Arnold's down there and it's a good program. They offer—and I think they will—you sign. The Marines will still be there after college, and you can join then."

"How'd you know I was gonna enlist?" I asked.

"How you think, Reaser?" said coach Arritt. "I got a call from your mom! You got her all worked up with some letter about this Marine Corps business. You wanna upset your mom?"

"No," I said.

"She wants to see her boy go to college."

"I understand."

"You can still join the Marines, Reaser. Jus' go to college first."

"Ok, Coach."

"Go on the Stetson visit. They're gonna offer you full ride down there. The whole package. They want you. So don't be ridiculous. The Marine Corps ain't goin' nowhere. Sign with Stetson, get you a degree, and enjoy Florida. It's what's best for you and it's what your mom wants, Reaser. Go to college. You can join the Marines later."

'nough said.

Stetson University

I took the official visit to Stetson, which was a nice getaway from FUMA—the type of institution that is only great in hindsight—landed in Orlando, disembarked, and met Assistant Coach Wylie Tucker in the airport lobby. When I walked outside and took in the Florida sun, the palm trees, the tropical breeze, I knew I wanted to go to Stetson. It did not matter that I had not yet seen the school nor had been to DeLand. Intuition is a strange and inexplicable thing, and for me, sometimes irresistible to a fault. Sometimes we *just know*, even if we really do not. We spend our life making choices based on hunches—*the feel* of a thing. Fact and reason are clothes we drape over decisions we have already made in the gut, the mind often a step behind the heart. It was a good visit, but I had already made up my mind. Stetson offered during the visit, and

I signed. The scramble to get to the college level was over. I was going to Stetson.

I arrived Stetson for my freshmen year, hoop dreams somewhat renewed—you never know—ready to work. I partied and had fun, but I was always ready to put in the work for the game. I took practice seriously and did what I had to do in my classes for school. Coach Arritt thought that Stetson would be a good fit for me because the Atlantic Sun Conference (then called the TAAC) was a small conference, which meant I would have a good chance to compete, get some playing time. It was a low-level Division I conference, which meant that Stetson could not compete with major conferences in the recruiting game.

Even more of a reason for me to go to Stetson, Coach Arritt said, was the head coach, Murray Arnold. Coach Arnold had been around the game for a long time. He had coached at Chattanooga and Western Kentucky. His players graduated.

His coaching style was a good fit for my game. It was a good fit conference wise and a good fit coach wise. It was all a player, such as myself, could ask for.

And for my freshmen year this proved to be true. I played in every game, and even started once. I was efficient with the minutes I was given. In one game, I scored ten points with eight minutes of playing time, turning the game around with two three-pointers, a baseline jumper, and two free throws. I fit well and played proficiently in Coach Arnold's system.

I felt I was playing as well as the upper classmen ahead of me in the rotation, but I understood that I was a freshman. I would keep grinding and putting in the work and my time was coming. Stetson was a good school. My classes were interesting. My professors were not just good teachers but also they were interesting people, down to earth. The school work was engaging and interesting. The classes were small, personal, and likeable. The social life was good; the weather was amazing. Daytona Beach was north of DeLand, Orlando to the west. Campus life was fun. I settled into the major of communication studies and minored in education because Coach Arritt had said, "Make sure you take some classes in education, Reaser. You can always fall back on a teaching job."

But the plotline of life is not without its twists and turns, and rarely do things work out as we would imagine. At the end of my freshmen year, Coach Arnold abruptly retired due to poor health conditions and *just like that*, the program I was recruited to play for was finished. As a role player, such change is a big deal and can mean the difference between playing and not playing. The really good players usually transfer, like Jason Williams did when Billy Donovan left Marshall for Florida, but I was not a great talent. Where was I going to transfer? I had already used my "redshirt" year at FUMA. And there was the fact that I liked Stetson. I liked DeLand. I liked my teachers. I liked the social life. I wanted to stay. I wanted things to work out, and I believe that I would still make it happen.

I was dead wrong about that, but because of faith in my abilities, and misplaced optimism, I tried. Derek Waugh got the head coaching job. He was twenty-nine years old at that time, making him the youngest Division I head coach in the country. When he took over the program, it was as if I fell off the roster. Any playing time I had simply vanished. Even if I played excellent in practice, it was to no avail. If I outplayed a player in his rotation, Waugh would simply get angry with that player.

I worked hard to earn playing time. When on-the-court success did not work (outplaying other players), I went to his office to speak with him, to try an understand what the problem was. He would give me what I felt to be a fabricated smile and say something that I suppose he thought was encouraging, a patent "keep working hard" with a pat on the back, showing me to the door. I got the feeling I was already written off early on.

It seemed to me that Waugh highly esteemed muscularity and the genetics of a natural athlete in a player. He favored players with superior athleticism, even if they did not have much of a basketball IQ. Players with both superior athleticism and a high basketball IQ did not seek to play in the Atlantic Sun Conference.

I was of average athletic ability among my Atlantic Sun Conference peers. I could dunk the basketball, but not in traffic. I did not have a big max on the bench press. I was not superfast or super quick, but I could hold my own. I was aware of my weaknesses but did not see why they put me out of the running for a chance to play. I could still outplay players with more athleticism in their DNA, and often did so in practice. Basketball, after all, was not a jumping contest. Having a huge max on the bench press did not mean that you could shoot or move without the ball.

Waugh recruited transfers to Stetson, players from mid-major Division I programs (Rice, Tulane, and Richmond) that were not happy with their playing time at their respective programs. He also brought in a junior college's transfer. Maybe he thought he was "stealing" from the bigtime? To this day, the man baffles me. Nothing he did makes any sense. These "steals" he recruited did not have to earn their position and playing time in the position I was playing and it seemed to be understood on arrival. Did he consider that there might have been a reason these guys didn't get playing time at their former program?

Stetson could not "steal" a recruit from a mid-major program, much less a major Division I program. The Atlantic Sun rarely had a player even play professionally overseas, much less get drafted. And out of those that did get drafted, a fraction actually made a roster for an NBA team. Stetson would never get the Corey Maggette of the game. Even the best players on my FUMA team would have never gone to the Atlantic Sun Conference. Even high school Brett Nelson would have never played for an Atlantic Sun Conference team. Such players had far better options.

In the realm of Division I, the winner of the Atlantic Sun Conference was a 16th seed in an NCAA tournament bracket (last place), and for Stetson, simply making the NCAA tournament— getting that last place spot—was cause for major celebration. When we played mid-major and major conference teams—like the Florida Gators—it was called a "guarantee game" in college parlance because the Gators were essentially guaranteed to win. How a "guarantee game" works is, the Gators athletic department would pay the Stetson athletic department around thirty thousand dollars (probably more money now), as well as our travel, hotel, and meals, to come play them on their home court so they could get a guaranteed win for an out-of-conference game. All things are not equal in Division I NCAA basketball.

Maybe Waugh figured he would get players with the athleticism of a major Division I recruit and then somehow impute the basketball IQ he would need to be able to win games? Maybe he thought he could get around the fact that Stetson would always have to recruit from the leftovers, and he could use players that knew their way around the court, even when playing against superior athletes? Maybe he did not understand how valuable the fundaments of the game were? What good would it be to have gifted athletes who thought they were better than they actually were?

Whatever Waugh was trying to do, it never manifested in a winning record. His anointed players could slam-dunk the basketball and/or were studs in the weight room, but winning games? Not so much. For the sake of writing this book, I did a little research on the internet to check out Waugh's record as the head coach at Stetson and was very disturbed to see that he is wrongly given credit for Murray Arnold's 2000–01 Stetson season, when we had a winning record of 17–12, and Coach Arnold retired for health reasons at the end of season. That was the year I played every game and even started for one game, as a freshman. Waugh would have never given me the kind of minutes I had when Coach Arnold was coaching. Waugh's first year to start the season was 2001–02, and we quickly dropped to a losing record of 10–16. The following year, after Waugh had all his athletic transfers, the 2002–03 team dropped to a losing record of 7–20. The 2003–04 season was 12–15, a little better than the year before, but still a losing season. I graduated and Waugh would go on to lead Stetson to a losing season until 2007–08, which would not exactly be a winning season but I suppose a 50%; 16–16 record would be a cause of celebration for Waugh.

I was disturbed to see that Waugh's Wikipedia page was written to make him look like a great coach. It says he "finished his career second in program history in all-time wins in 2011," making him look like he was a "winner." In a limited view, this is technically true because he won 125 games, but it is tremendously misleading. He might have won 125 games, but that was out of the 321 games he was surprisingly allowed to continue to coach. I made a list of all the basketball coaches in the history of Stetson (from online searches), checked the records, and out of the twenty-one coaches I found, sixteen of them had a winning percentage of 40% or above. Derek Waugh was *not* one of them. In terms of coaches in the history of Stetson basketball, Derek Waugh is in the top five for the worst "winning" percentage of all times at 39%, and that is from rounding up. With a "winning" percentage of 39%, he remains one of the worst basketball coaches in the history of the University, and given that he was allowed to coach an astounding 321 games while losing nearly 200 of those games, he was the longest loser of all the coaches by many miles. That he was allowed to keep his job in a usually pressurized, cut-throat atmosphere as Division I NCAA men's basketball, while losing at such a steady rate, is baffling. For Waugh to be placed second to Glenn Wilkes is criminal. Wilkes had a winning percentage of 56% out of 987 games. Waugh was able to win 125 games because he was allowed to keep losing over a ten-year span. Furthermore, Waugh was given the seventeen wins from the 2000–01 winning season, which truly belonged to Murray Arnold, as Waugh took over on the tail end of that season.

In a small way, I had been prepared for something like this because Coach Arritt had warned us about the possibility of something like this happening; "Happens all the time," he had said. The coach that recruited you retires, leaves for a better coaching job, and a new coach comes in, bring new players with him. I reached out to Coach Arritt and he reminded me that what was happening to me happened to players all the time each year in college. Even in the pros, a coaching change can make or break a career. "That's why you gotta get your degree!" Coach Arritt told me. He reminded me that in the end it is all about getting the degree, so just keep up with the school work and do what you have to do.

I did, but still, it seemed to get worse with each day. My sophomore season, Waugh's true first season, he cut the minutes I had as a freshman—ten to fifteen minutes at least—down to two or three minute per game with no explanation or reason given. It would be one thing if the players he brought in were better, or we were winning more games, but our record

121

tanked. The season was abysmal. We started losing.

To make matter worse for me, there was no scenario where I could compete for playing time. With Waugh, I often did not even get to play in practice. I would spend a vast majority of practice just standing on the sideline, as if I were not even good enough to play on the second-string team. For a player that played every game as a freshman, sometimes scoring in double figures, and even starting for a game—in the only winning season we had out of my four years—this made no sense. Waugh went on to not only knock me out of the rotation, he benched me as if I had never proved myself.

The minutes he gave me were patronizing, like the minute I got in the sixth grade that ignited my fire to get better. But in the sixth grade it made sense. The player that played ahead of me was better. He had been playing on a team with the same guys for years. But with Waugh, it seemed to be for no other reason than his fancy.

And those one to two minutes per game as a sophomore would be the best I would ever get from Waugh. After that, I was finished. During my junior and senior year, I would not play at all, just ride the bench the entire time. It would be one thing if he would have matched me up in practice against the players I could compete with for playing time and I was outplayed, but that never happened. That is the way it is supposed to be. What coach could not understand that? If I was clearly outplayed, I would have understood. But I would sometimes get to play with the second string, and we would often beat the starters in scrimmages.

With Waugh, the first team would not only lose most of the regular season games but they would lose in practice as well. Any other half-decent coach I had ever played for would have started using different lineups, giving other players a chance. That would have helped his beloved to play better. But instead of changing his rotation—when his chosen played poorly—Waugh would just get mad at his chosen and throw fits.

My last two years of college basketball were totally misery for me. I got to the point where I was glad he did not put me in the game, and I might have refused to go in if he had tried. I did not want his charity. It was a terrible team and we almost always lost. The attitudes were dreadful, including mine. One practice, as the starters were getting their asses kicked by the second team, Waugh threw a tantrum and punted a basketball into the rafters and kicked us all out of the gym. In the locker room, as the players hung their heads, I tried to lift the bad vibe. The whole scene was nuts. But some of his beloved players—who seemingly did not have to earn playing time—snapped back at me. I let it go. I was on the team, but not of it. That such foolishness could be allowed to go on at the Division I NCAA level—even if it was a low-level conference—for that many years will forever remain dumbfounding.

I came to hate every moment around the team. I wanted to quit so bad. Then I felt that the scholarship was not worth it. Now I realize that I was incorrect for thinking that, but that is what I believed at the time. But because of Mom and her desire to see me graduate, I stuck it out, but I was walking a very thin line. I had a way out—the Marine Corps. I started talking to a local Marine Corps recruiter in DeLand during my junior year and came very close to enlisting and quitting college altogether.

Mom seemed to sense it and would call and encourage me to just hang in there and get a college degree. It was miserable. I used alcohol to help me get through it. I would drink a little throughout the day and before practice or a game and then more in the evening. Only through intoxication I felt the courage to keep going to the circus. There were other players who were having trouble as well. Mark Stiles was a fellow teammate who for reasons unknown to him found his progression moving backwards. After a decent sophomore year, averaging ten ppg and five rpg, he lost favor with Waugh, and his playing time cut in half.

Mark Stiles' fall from grace was strange to me because he was a year behind me, a player recruited with Waugh as the head coach. But Stiles was out of high school, and Waugh seemed to favor transfers with more relish, so perhaps that had something to do with it. Plus, Stiles did not have the bulky stature that Waugh seemed to favor, so that could have been the problem as well. But that was the problem with Waugh: *it was never clear*. Basketball for him was no meritocracy. He did not run a merit system, so it was impossible to know how to get his blessing. It was not working hard, playing will, or winning basketball games—I had proven that. It was a situation that simply sucked. We just kept losing and he would get mad and throw tantrum, but he never adjusted, never changed. I eventually realized that it was better not to think about it because it would just drive you crazy. I would just get through it and get the degree.

Stiles kept working his ass off, trying to win back his playing time, I figured Waugh for more of a GM union foreman than a basketball coach. He might get mad and yell, but he did not bench his beloved.

It was another situation that FUMA inadvertently prepared me for, mainly how to suck it up and deal with the daily grind. But at FUMA, I at least had basketball. At Stetson, basketball was paying the bill for college, but it was also the source of my misery. Craig Butts and Derrick Rogers turned out to be the smart players of my recruiting class because they transferred out. I do not know what came of Rogers, but Craig Butts, who saw that there was no hope with Derek Waugh early on, transferred to Clayton State. Like me, Butts had come in under Murray Arnold. Butts knew Waugh would never give him playing time and he left and went to Clayton and played in every game, and started every game his senior year. Not only that, he did something that he never would have been able to do at Stetson: play for a winning team. Butts ended his college playing career with an 18–13 record.

But like I said before, we often live life more according to instinct and intuition than facts and figures, and for whatever the reasons, I felt like I was supposed to be at Stetson. I stuck it out. I would have moments of clarity and put away the booze and dig deeper into my studies. I had some excellent professors. In all my time at Stetson, I cannot remember one teacher I did not like. They were all very good, some standing out in my mind more than others. I realized that I had to simply deal with the basketball nonsense and get my degree. I was not going to be playing pro ball anyway. Stetson was a good school, and DeLand was a nice place to live.

Dr. Charles "Chuck" Vedder was one of my favorite teachers. I had him for sociology and criminology, and he put me on to books such as *One Flew Over the Cuckoo's Nest* by Ken Kesey, *Hell's Angels: The Strange and Terrible Saga of the Outlaw Motorcycle Gangs* by Hunter S. Thompson, *The Electric Kool-Aid Acid Test* by Tom Wolfe, *The Stranger Beside Me* by Ann Rule, and *Mindhunter: Inside the FBI's Elite Serial Crime Unit* by John E. Douglas and Mark Olshaker. These books opened my mind to different ways of thinking.

Michael McFarland was another teacher that enlightened my perspective. I had him for a class called extremism, in which—among other things—we studied literature of extremist groups. He showed us how the Aryan Nations interpreted the "mark of Cain" in the Bible and used it as a foundation for establishing white supremacy, and how fictions like *The Turner Diaries*—which we read—were used to influence thinking. He talked about the subtle snake-like reasoning behind racism, how literature and philosophy played an important role in developing the rational, and how so many people fell victim to charms of those who peddled it.

Dr. Philip Dalton was like my writing enforcer. He was always pushing me to do a better job, handing back marked up papers I had written and giving me the guidance for what he expected. I had only started writing at FUMA, and even then, all informal. When I arrived at Stetson, I had never attempted any kind of formal writing. Were it not for FUMA, I would have really been in trouble. My professors saw me as a struggling writer lacking grammar, structure, and everything in between. If they only knew! I had actually improved a great deal since high school.

I do not blame my former teachers. I was a terrible student. I would not have listened if they did teach me everything I needed to know. Now that I was at Stetson, and was going through devastation with respect to basketball, I was ready to learn something new. So I was ready to listen. I did not have any sense of the structure required for academic writing, but Dr. Dalton would use class time to backtrack and teach some of the basic structural elements, starting with the simple technique of the five-paragraph essay. It is amazing how deficient I was with respect to the most basic writing fundamentals. I struggled with it but once my teachers saw that I was serious about getting better, made the changes they recommended, and I was coming from a lack of writing experience, they took the time to work with me and my skill improved to an acceptable level.

The teachers at Stetson gave me plenty of things, other than basketball, to occupy my mind. They were interesting people that were serious and passionate about their discipline. They were students themselves. They had questions, talked about current events, and were interested in the students in front of them. They were people that you wanted to be like. They were smart, interesting, and into reading between the lines, looking not just on the surface of a thing but below as well.

But it was still tough to deal with the heartbreak of what was happening in basketball. After all the hard work and time that I had put into the game and all the great coaches I had played for, how could it end like this? What was the lesson? What was the point? I had been living and dealing with heartbreak for so long but now in basketball? Basketball was the one place I had where I could get away from the stress, and now it was the source of it? How could this happen? I would learn the answers later, but I did not have a clue at the time. The problem was never Waugh; the problem was always me and my struggle with reconciling my reality with the identity I had worked so hard to cultivate. "Those who have a false opinion of themselves," wrote Montaigne, "can feed on false approbations . . ."

I made up my mind to enlist in the Marines, but I would wait until after I graduated. I would hang in there and get through it, take it day-by-day, and make it to graduation. When the second semester of my senior year started, I sought out the athletic director of Stetson and spoke to him frankly about my situation. I want to know if I could quit the team and still graduate without having to financially pay back the school for the last semester. What was the point for me to finish out the year? I was no good to the team and I was barely hanging on emotionally. I told him about my life in high school, and how I was only sticking this out for Mom so she would see me graduate. I told him how I could not get myself to practice or show up to a game without first drinking a few shots of whiskey, which was how I truly felt at the time. I do not remember what all I said. I did not prepare or write anything down prematurely; I spoke for the heart, the gut.

Whatever I said, it worked. The AD gave me the green light to call it quits on the basketball team. I think he could tell that I was being genuine and sincere and that it truly was better for everybody involved for me to not be on the team. It was such a relief. It was a sad kind of relief, because I loved the game, but I needed to graduate, and I do not know if I could have pulled it together academically that last semester if I had to keep dealing with Waugh. I had fallen behind my senior year, drinking to excess more often than not, dulling the pain with alcohol. I really would have quit if it were not for Mom planning to see me walk across the stage.

And I did graduate. Shedding the basketball obligations gave me ample time to catch up on missing assignment and get done what I needed to get done in order to graduate. Now I could concentrate on school. The desire to drink to excess dissipated. Mom made plans to come to my graduation and brought my sister, Jaime, along with her. Mom was happier about my graduation from college than I was.

Seeing Jaime was a hard blow. She was having some serious health issues. Jaime had been diagnosed with multiple sclerosis years earlier, but the disease was worse and continuing to get worse. Her marriage was falling apart as well, and she was now sharing an apartment with Mom in Manhattan. There was not anything I could do about any of that, so I tried not to think about it. I had already signed the enlistment contract and I would be leaving for Parris Island soon.

After the graduation, Mom, Jaime, and I spent some time together before they went back to New York. They could not understand why I would want to enlist. They thought I should at least try to go in as an officer. Looking back, I have no idea why I thought the way I did. For some reason, I figured I did not want to be an officer. I wanted to enlist. Why? Sometimes there are no answers to these things.

This time I would follow through with it; I enlisted in the Marine Corps. I had come close to doing it thrice before: once during my senior year of high school, once at the end of FUMA, and once during my junior year at Stetson. But I did not follow through with it because of the opportunity to play basketball and then Mom's expressed desire to see me graduate college. Now there was nothing in the way. I had graduated from college and basketball was finished. I did not have a job, nor did I have any idea what I would do if I did not enlist. I did not have any desire to do anything other than enlist in the Marines.

When I knew I had my graduation in the bag, before the actual ceremony, I worked out a four-year enlistment contract with a guaranteed logistics MOS (Marine Occupation Specialty) upon graduating recruit training. My shipping date was set for a few weeks after my college graduation. This way, before I left for Parris Island, Mom and Jaime could see me walk across the stage and we could spend some time together. But there was nowhere else I wanted to go, and nowhere else I wanted to be. It was time to say bye to the civilian world.

The Marine Corps

Oh, God, I thought to myself, *I've made a terrible mistake!* What had I been thinking? I volunteered for this? Surely there is a way out of this! This cannot be happening!

It *was* happening. The first two or three days were a blur. I was going through the motions, trying to cope with the abrupt change and abrasive culture. The blur started to come into focus when I was assigned to a platoon and met the drill instructors that were to train me. Then the real hell broke loose. Everything that was happening struck me as absolute madness. Now I was a recruit, training on Parris Island, Bravo Company, platoon 2077. Culture shock is hardly a sufficient description for the jolt I was experiencing. At first, it was mentally paralyzing. Sometimes I would find myself staring into space, trying to figure out what in God's name had I gotten myself into, only to be brought back into my hard reality by a drill instructor.

The Marine Corps drill instructor (DI) was, to me, a new breed of the human species, and to this day he remains one of the most unique types I have ever encountered. They were everywhere; DIs ruled Parris Island. They were walking thunderstorms, compact and razor sharp. What planet did these guys come from? I had stepped off the face of the earth and landed in a world of gray, olive drab squad bays, sandpits, parade decks, and DIs striding about in campaign covers, emanating ferocity. Later, when I got to the fleet, I talked to some former DIs.

"How do you do it?" I asked.

"What do you mean?" asked the former DI.

"Keep up that intensity? It's like you never eat or sleep. Yet you're always savagely energized and your uniform is always perfect."

"Shit, devil dog, we just rotate. Give each other breaks. The recruits don't see the breaks.

139

While one of us would be drilling the platoon or whatever, the other would be hideout, eating a hot dog or whatever. We never let the recruits see us eat or relax. That was part of the show."

They did a great job of it. There was never a moment when a DI was not intense and on some demon time.

After a few days with my platoon, I thought I would see if I could get out of this mess I had put myself in. I requested permission to speak with the senior DI, who was the only DI somewhat approachable, like the father of the platoon. When I got a chance to speak, the conversation was short. It was in his office, and it was only the two of us.

"What do you want, recruit?" asked the senior DI.

"I've made a mistake," I said. "I shouldn't have enlisted."

"This recruit! This recruit! Are you fucking slow?"

I gathered myself and rephrased: "*This recruit has made a mistake. This recruit* should not have enlisted."

"Now you listen to me, recruit, and you listen good. Graduation is the only way off my island. Get the fuck outta my sight."

I froze, wanting to say more, standing there at ridged attention but not knowing what to do. After about three uncomfortable beats, he leapt up from behind his desk, shoved me out his office door, and commenced to "smoke" me on the quarterdeck.

I accepted my fate. My entire focus became centered around one thought: graduating and getting the hell off of Parris Island. I had to get through recruit training. But that goal was too far away and depressing to think about. I needed simple goals within reach that would help me get through the day. Upon reveille, my goal would be to make it to breakfast chow. After accomplishing that goal, it would be to make it to the afternoon chow. Upon accomplishing that goal, it would be making it to the evening chow. Then, after accomplishing that goal, I would try to make it to that glorious moment when the lights would go out, and I could mark of another day off my calendar and just lay there in a moment of peace and quiet and drift off into sleep. The next day, I would do it again.

In the early days of the first phase of recruit training, I was not the only recruit that felt he had made a mistake by enlisting. The DIs—knowing that a number of us wanted to go back in time and forget this whole misunderstanding—threatened that if we wanted to play the "crying game," they would keep us on the island even longer, far past the graduation date of the platoon to which we were currently assigned.

One DI would say, "You wanna play games, recruit? We can play games. I've got more games than Milton Bradley." The "game" was, supposedly—I never pushed the envelope to find out—that if we did not go along, the DIs would send us to the "head shrinker" and then to a sick bay, where we would be stuck until we were "better" and then recycled into a new incoming platoon, thus, moving our graduation date back, keeping us on the island even longer. The fastest way off the island, they said, was to *suck it the fuck up*, fall in line, and graduate.

I accepted it. What could I do? It was not that recruit training was hard, it all just seemed insane. I had gone into Parris Island blind. I had not reviewed any of the preparation material my recruiter had given me. I figured being in good physical condition was the only thing that mattered. I had not prepared myself beyond that; I did not think I needed to. How hard could it be?

It was more challenging, but in ways I did not expect. Like speaking in the third person. I could never say "I," as in, "I have to go to the bathroom." I had to refer to myself as, "this recruit." Being older and educated (in the arts and liberal sense) was a terrible disadvantage in recruit training. Questions, asking why, reflection, thinking and considering, were things caused you to hesitate, which was not a helpful characteristic for a recruit. Thinking about "why" gave pause to instant obedience. At first, I could not help myself, and the urge to laugh would haunt me. Speaking in third person was such a strange way of communicating. Were it not for having to use the bathroom, I would not have ever tried to speak to the DIs. But I did, and so I would first have to request permission to speak and then ask the question upon approval. There were no raising hands, just shouting in a loud, aggressive, commanding voice.

"Sir, good afternoon, sir! This recruit requests permission *to speak* to drill instructor, Sgt. Fields, sir!"

If permission was denied, I would have to try again until the DI was satisfied with how I requested permission. What you had to do, basically, was talk like the drill instructor: loud, intense, and with that bold confidence that only a DI projects. By way of not approving my permission to speak, the DI would say something like, "Why are you talking sweet to me? Am I wearing lipstick? Do you see me with a dress on?"

And I would try again. Once permission is granted, you continue: "This recruit requests permission to use the head, sir!"

I would, of course, never say "bathroom." I had to learn a new vernacular for the sake of the Marine Corps "naval traditions." Our entire squad bay was loosely modeled after the deck of a ship: quarterdeck, starboard, and port side, aft.

The quarterdeck is where the individual recruit would often get "smoked." To be smoked was to be put through a relentless session of pushups, mountain climbers, side-straddle hops, etc. until you could not go any longer, that is, until you were smoked. But to me, getting smoked was almost comforting, as it symbolized the relationship between Dad and me during basketball workouts. The physical fitness part of recruit training was not near as difficult as nailing down the speaking patterns. But I did get accustomed to speaking in the third person. What I was never about to get used to was the never-ending drill.

Everything revolved around drill, and drill never got comfortable. Standing stoically at attention, marching, right-facing, left-facing, right-shoulder-arming, left-shoulder-arming, flanking, to-the-rear-marching, driving the heel of *this recruit's* boot into the ground, hands tightly gripping *this recruit's* rifle. Drill was not limited to the parade grounds; we went to bed by command, woke up by command, put on clothes by command, cleaned, showered, exercised, ate, and studied—all by command.

The military defines drill as "the preparation of Marines for performance of their duties in peace and war through the practice and rehearsal of prescribed movements . . . drill consolidates soldiers into battle formations and familiarizes them with their weapons. Psychologically, it develops a sense of teamwork, discipline, and self-control; it promotes automatic performance of duties under disturbing circumstances and instinctive response to the control and stimulus of leaders." My layman's definition of drill is: how a drill instructor psychologically takes over the recruit, replacing the recruit's personal inner voice with his own. You move on command; you halt on command. Everything you do is by command.

And there was a kind of history education we had. I was surprised by the number of things we had to memorize. Aside from the Bible—a pocket Gideon New Testament with Psalms and Proverbs in the back—the only "book" you were to have, *required to have on your person at all times*, was a small book (a pamphlet, really) that the DIs called "your knowledge."

Any time we would be waiting for some reason or another (hurry up and wait), the drill instructor would say, "Get out your knowledge," and we would all say, "Aye, sir!" and hastily reach into our cargo pocket—where *this recruit's* knowledge had *better be*—and remove it from its water-proofing bag and quietly study its contents: General Orders, the "naval tradition" vernacular, enlisted and officer rank structure for the Marine Corps and the Navy, names and dates of important military figures, events, wars, the nomenclature for the M16A2 service rifle, etc. On this knowledge we were tested with regularity. Often the DI would shout questions and we would chant the answer back in unison, which was a surprisingly effective way for memorization.

Every night I continued to enjoy marking off a day on my small calendar, a piece of paper with three months fit into three small rectangles. Marking off a day was always a spectacular moment, counting down, dreaming of the day when I could get off Parris Island. Beside each day I numbered a countdown so I could see how many days I had left to graduation at the end of each day. I eventually figured out that the DIs were somewhat bullshitting about recruits not being able to get off Parris Island without graduating. Our platoon had shrunk from 70-some recruits to 50. The DIs were making their own decisions between the recruits that did not *like it* from those with genuine head problems. *Whatever,* I thought. *I would just stick it out.*

Recruit life was Groundhog Day—same thing over and over—until the rifle range, which we went to during our third and final month. There we had to qualify with our rifle at minimum for a "marksman" badge, the lowest of three qualifications. The next level was "sharpshooter," and the best was "expert." We had to qualify from distances of hundred and 200 yards in three shooting positions—sitting, kneeling, and standing—and from 500 yards in the prone position.

We had to do this without a scope or any other assistive technology. We had to establish our BZO—Battlesight Zero—from 20-yards out and then adjust our weapon accordingly, using sight alignment, sight picture, front and rear-sight apertures, and move groupings to center-mass, making notation in a riffle notebook.

From the 500-yard line, laying prone under a hot sun, we had to use our hand (opposite the trigger hand) as a support to steady the muzzle of the rifle. To turn our hand into a firm, unmoving buttress, we used the rifle sling to cut off the blood circulation at the upper arm (like how a junky will tie off his arm to find a vein), elbow grounded, making the guide hand as still and steady as an inanimate object after the first few uncomfortable moments. After your hand goes to sleep, it goes numb, and you get used to it. It works well.

Below the targets being shot at, on the other side of the firing range, was another story. While one group of Marines was on the firing line, shooting, the other group was underneath the targets, looking up, watching so they would be able to mark the target where round struck. When a round would strike through the target, we would pull the target down and place a marker in the fresh hole and then send the target back up so the shooter could make notation in his rifle notebook of where his round struck the target. We would tie the targets up on a frame with a pulley system, which allowed us to raise the target above the berm: the only thing between us and the rounds being fired.

The targets were big, and we would have to prepare them in working parties. We would have to stick a paper target on large canvases attached to wooden frames. First, we would swab the canvas with a glue-like substance and then stick the target onto the canvases. It was hard work. Marines would be back behind that berm, hundreds of rounds flying just over head, making targets, hoisting them up, pulling them down, working like ants in a colony.

The shooting at the rifle range was the first thing I enjoyed and found interesting since day one of recruit training. I was good at it, even though I had never been hunting or seriously fired a rifle for accuracy. The rifle range was a break from the monotony, and at the range, the DIs were more passive, relaxed. And they could be because we were third-phase recruits. We knew what to do, how to march, speak, etc. Out on the rifle range, finally having live rounds, working on our marksmanship, the purpose of recruit training started to come together. We were getting closer to graduation and started to feel like Marines. We started to feel "badass."

Coming back from rifle range—we camped out there for two weeks—to our company barracks, we started taking more pride and gaining confidence as a platoon. We found ourself marching past first-phase recruits with aggressiveness. *We're third phase, motherfuckers, don't fuck with us.* We had become good at drilling. When the platoon marched, it was as if one loud boot smacked the ground with each step. It was like a thunderous boom. In rifle manual, as we marched, each hand would smack the weapon in unison, making a thunderous clap. Our DI began not just to call the cadence, but sing it. The prospect of graduating and finally becoming a Marine started to mean something that was indescribable.

The more I began to identify myself as a Marine, the less I thought and reflected on basketball. Recruit training had marked the first time since the sixth grade that I had not just spent an entire day but *three months* without my hands touching a basketball. I never even saw a basketball for the entire duration of time I spent on Parris Island. There had not been a single day—that I can recall—where I had not worked on improving my game, often beyond whatever I had done during a team practice, sometimes shooting upwards of one thousand jump shots and hundred free throws in a single workout session, day after day. Even in bed I would often lie facing the ceiling, fingers spread on a basketball, flicking my wrist, absentmindedly watching the rotation of the basketball as I practice my form before falling asleep. Even after my sophomore season at Stetson when I was not getting any more playing time and had begun to divert my attention to other walks of life—social and academic—I would still find a place to leisurely shoot around, toss up some shots as I would think things over.

Basketball had long been a kind of sanctuary for me, a sacred place where I could clear my mind of all the bullshit in life and concentrate on the game. I would shoot and zone out—*front edge of the rim, fingertip control, ball in the alley*— one shot after another, careful not to practice missing. Even as my college career was winding up, and after nights of hard drinking, I would often find a hoop to shoot some free throws under the moon's reflection as I tried to simply hold it together in a crazy, unfair world. I had been living in pursuit of hoop dreams for my entire life, and now I was in recruit training, learning to develop a new identity. For me, it was a big deal.

Graduating the three months of recruit training felt like more of an accomplishment than four years of undergraduate college. After graduating college, I felt a kind of despair because basketball was officially finished for me and I had no idea how to reinvent myself. The tools for change were made available through the academics, but for whatever reason, I was not ready to take ahold of them. I was still blind and stubbornly stuck in my hoop dreams. I could not take pride in my academic accomplishments and use the new things I was learning to establish a new identity for myself. I did not graduate college for me; I was graduating college for Mom. I did not care. I was graduating from recruit training on Parris Island for me, and that was where I found some pride, self-confidence, and a new identity that I had earned through the training. I was able to accomplish more with respect to personal maturity and character development in those three months than I was in four years of college.

When my DIs finally addressed me as a marine, it felt excellent. I had a new focus in life. I was a marine, and even though I did not know exactly what that meant, it did not matter: I had a new identity. That I never had gotten closure on a life dedicated to basketball did not matter. I had not made it in basketball, but now I could let it go. I was finally over it. No more *trying to make it*. I had nothing else to prove. It was as if I had finally escaped my childhood.

Through TVCS, Saint Albans, Morgantown, back to Saint Albans, FUMA, and Stetson, I was just trying to survive and keep from sinking into despair. Basketball was the only thing I could find to hold on to. I had to believe in my hoop dreams. They were the only thing that motivated me to keep going to my classes, to keep stepping one foot in front of the other, to keep moving forward. Believing in my hoop dreams had taken on a religious vibe: I just had to keep believing. It is like the religious faith healer who says you are not healed because you lack faith. That same element of mysticism had crept into my believing I could make it to the NBA. Even when it became clear that that was not going to happen, *I had to keep the faith*. If I could only *just believe*.

But it was never about basketball. It was always about surviving and staying strong. It was about finding something to keep me from staying blind drunk. It was about finding a way to get through Mom's cries. But it took me a long time to see what was really happening. At Stetson, when everything began to fall apart, it was convenient to simply blame Derrek Waugh. I will always believe he was a terrible basketball coach, but that is beside the point. If my goals in life fell apart when a man like Derrek Waugh got in the way then the problem was with *me* and my ability to set appropriate goals for myself.

I had not yet learned to rationally consider what kind of expectations and goals I was creating for myself. It was like I was going through life as if I had been pushed of a precipice: when you are falling it does not matter who pushed you, or how you were knocked off, you are still going to be falling until you hit the bottom. That bottom, for me, was recruit training. There, I learned to set realistic goals for myself (make it to breakfast chow) and accomplish them (take a moment for self-congratulations, deep breath, eat) and then move to the next goal (make it to afternoon chow). In recruit training, I learned how to live, which is basically the process of taking one step after the next, moving from moment to moment, meal to meal, handling the responsibilities in front of you. When you can line up these simple goals in a positive direction that works for you, you have learned how to live your best life.

After recruit training, I had gotten the Eagle, Globe, and Anchor. My DIs congratulated me and addressed me as a marine. It was over. I left Parris Island with Mom and Jaime. I had a week of liberty before I had to report to MCT (Marine Combat Training) in NC, then my MOS (Marine Occupation Specialty) school for logistics— embarkation specialist—also in NC.

I would deal with that later. For the moment, I was getting a break, and I was leaving Parris Island. Outside the gates, I picked up a forty-ounce bottle of Budweiser and a pack of cigarettes. Mom was driving, Jaime was riding shotgun. They did all the talking. I just sat in the backseat, sipping my beer, smoking a cigarette, these taking me high as a kite after three months of total abstinence. At that point, a Snickers bar and soda would have gotten me high. I had to put out the cigarette because Mom did not like me smoking. She did not say anything but I could see it in her face. The beer was good enough. After a little driving, at a stop sign, I looked out the window and saw some guys shooting around, playing basketball in a park. My brows furrowed; my concentration came into focus.

"Pull over," I said.

"What?" Mom said.

"Just pull over. I need get out the car real quick."

Mom pulled over and I got out and walked to the court. I went to the rim where a young man was shooting on a goal.

"Hey, man," I said. "Lemme get a shot."

"You just finished boot camp?"

I was still in my alphas, no jacket. "Recruit training. Yeah."

"Here you go."

He passed me the ball. I took a shot from the wing, just inside the three-point line.

Nothing but net.

Basketball Resurrected in a Most Peculiar Way

MCT was a month of camping and training in the woods of Camp Geiger, NC. It was basically a 101 in combat training—*every Marine is a rifleman*—for marines with a noncombat MOS. Marines with a non-combat MOS get an abbreviated one-month combat course and then we move on to our MOS school to learn the basics of our job. Marines with a combat MOS do not go to MCT, they go to ITB (Infantry Training Battalion), which is longer and far more in-depth training for combat.

My school, for embarkation specialists, was short of two months, also in NC, on Camp Johnson, NC. Camp Johnson was a base for Logistics Operations School—combat service support—and guess what was a popular pastime every evening on Camp Johnson?

Basketball.

The job was straightforward. The coursework covered a variety of transport vessels, logistical equipment, and how to use load planning software. Embarkers were like the Marine Corps in house moving company: planning, packing, loading the gear, deploying. I would imagine the training for any shipyard or warehouse, UPS, FedEx, or Amazon to be somewhat similar. There was no need for a rifle. Barrack life was more like it was at FUMA than it was at recruit training or MCT, and even better: we had more time for ourselves.

School started around 8:00 am, and we were usually done for the day by 4:30 pm. Afterward, I would be in the field house playing basketball. In some ways it was like high school, but never any homework. Anything school related we learned and performed during class. Trade education is far more "cut-and-dry" than education in the realms of the arts and liberal.

The former is practical while the latter is abstract. Trade education is not about what you think, how you feel, or what your perspective is on an "issue." There are correct, practical, and efficient ways to do a job. There are tools to use, and here is how you use them. There was some math, but not the algebraic abstractions you are taught from middle school through college that serve very little practical purpose in the real world. Boxes and containers have certain dimensions and there is only so much square footage available per vessel or container. Certain vessels hold certain weight. When the math serves an actual purpose, and learning the computations and calculations help you load a vessel faster and correctly, therefore getting you a longer break—or out of school early—they are much easier to understand. Nobody has a "learned disability" and there is no "special ed."

We would get the job for the day done, and afterwards I was off to the gym. I would play for hours. The Marine Corps was big on sports. The athletic facilities on base were excellent: first-rate weight rooms, indoor lap pool, fields with baseball diamonds, and yard markers for football, soccer, etc. More importantly, in my case, gymnasiums for basketball.

The competition was surprisingly good. There were a few former All-Marine and All-Armed forces basketball players were stationed on Camp Johnson. The games were in the universal open-gym/streetball style: five-on-five, somebody calls "next," call your own fouls, winner stays up. With no more pressure, no feeling of *I have got to make it*, no self-imposed burden, I was playing more relaxed and creative, improvising in ways I never had, playing hard and just letting it happen. Nobody knew anything about me, my past, my pursuit of the game, my humiliating end at Stetson—I was just some Marine that could play good basketball.

Sometimes you have to be freed from certain pressures to realize they were actually there. Pressure that has long since become a weight you have been carrying for so long that you are unaware that it is there, indeed, unaware that there is a tremendous load on your shoulders, holding you down and disrupting your balance and flow, essentially obstructing your creativity. Now that I was in MOS school, I felt free from all those haunting pressures to survive—to make it—that had been plaguing me for so long. After Dad left, money had always been a problem. Simple things like having to make sure we had money for gas and groceries was always an issue. Things like this translated to me feeling that every time I played basketball, I had to prove that I was climbing the ladder to the NBA. I felt that basketball was my best talent, and NBA players made a lot of money. Therefore, I had to get a scholarship. Without a scholarship, there would be no college, and without college, there would be no NBA. So I would get a scholarship, make it to the NBA, and all of our financial worries would be over. *Hoop dreams*. And I held to the dream with everything I had because it was all I could see to hold on to.

But now, in the Marines, none of that mattered. I was far away from Mom and Dad, and I was living a nice and easy life compared to what I had been going through. Not that the pay was all that in the Marines. My salary was small. But I had no bills. I stayed in the barracks, I ate in the chow hall, and I spent hardly any money. I did not buy a car or cell phone. I did not need one. On base, everything was taken care of. There were restrictions about how far you could leave base, but I had nowhere else to be, so I felt free. For the first time, I could simply live in the moment and not worry about what I was going to do next. For the first time I could remember, when I played basketball, I could simply enjoy myself.

I was playing in a way that I never had before, and never better. I could handle the ball, direct traffic—pushing the tempo—slow it down, all in a light, relaxed way. I no long cared about making mistakes, and ironically, made less of them. Nothing mattered besides playing and having fun. I had been carrying such a heavy load, and the freedom from playing a part that was not *me* was a miraculous feeling. I had needed to get away from the game, and get some financial independence. After I had that and was given the opportunity to come back to the game, I was a different person with a different mentality.

As it turned out, basketball was an important aspect of the Marine Corps. In what is nothing less than mystical to me, I was able to have a worthy denouement—in the Marines—to a life of dedication to the game of basketball. It was not something that I could have planned, and how things turned out goes to show that while we can put in the work, we often have no way of knowing how the rewards of our work will manifest. All we can do is keep grinding and hope for the best.

For the next two years, I would, for the most part, play the best basketball of my career in the Marines. The opportunity was like a gift from the heavens. I would get as many as four consecutive months of temporary duty orders to play the game, making basketball my job during that time. In that sense, I was a professional basketball player in that I was getting paid to play. It was an odd and unexpected way to reach my hoop dreams, but I would take it.

All the hard work I put into the game of basketball paid off in the Marine Corps. I realized that it paid off by my getting a college degree in hindsight, but for a young man, hoop dreams are not about education, they are about the dream— getting paid to play basketball. It was not *education* that motivated me to shoot one thousand jump shots and hundred free throws, jump rope, and run every day. It was not *education* that motivated me to tip the basketball on the backboard hundred times with the right and left hand to improve my timing. It was not *education* that motivated me to push through the pain, and then push a little more.

What motivated me to push myself was the ambition to be the best, to have a powerful presence on the floor *during the game*, to earn and have the reputation of *being a player*. I wanted that status. Having been forced to give that up in failure after working so hard was devastating. Even though the reconciliation I would get in the Marines was nothing like the *real pros*, or the *real money* pros get, I would be very grateful and happy with what I got.

By the time my MOS training had come to an end, staff NCOs and officers were talking to me about playing for the All-Marine basketball team. There would be some steps involved, but I was on my way. The Marines that had made it into All-Marine sports were a small community. My standout game performance had reached the ears of some veterans of the All-Marine basketball team, that were now older and high rank, stationed at Camp Johnson. These Marines mentored me and explained the process. Our love for basketball brought us together. When I got my orders, the vets let me know who to contact when I touched down. Basketball was once again a part of my life.

Okinawa

The first orders I was cut were to the first MAW (Marine Aircraft Wing) in Okinawa, Japan, to MTACS-18 (Marine Tactical Air Command Squadron). As far as the Marine Corps culture goes, it was a fairly laid-back command. As long as you did what you had to do, and did not cause problems, you were treated with respect and life was smooth. Its mission: "to provide equipment, maintenance, and operations for the Tactical Air Command Center (TACC) of the Aviation Combat Element (ACE), as a component of the Marine Air-Ground Task Force (MAGTF). Equip, man, operate, and maintain the Current Operations section of the TACC."

I arrived, settled in, and got acquainted with my superiors and responsibilities. Appearance is everything in the Marines, and I wanted to get approval to play basketball, so I made sure to check in with my uniform sharp, in top physical condition, playing the part, which was an unspoken signaling to my superiors that they did not have to worry about me: I was not going to make trouble, and I could take care of myself. The Marines that had trouble with their weight or did not display the expected military bearing or lacked attention to detail with respect to the care of their uniform got the unwanted attention.

I did not want any extra attention because wanted all the time I could get to myself so I could check out the basketball scene. I was living on Camp Futenma. There was a nice indoor basketball court there, but the games were not all that competitive. I had been told back at Camp Johnson that Camp Foster was where the competitive games were. I was not yet allowed to leave the base on my own yet—and venture out into Okinawa—but there was a shuttle that I could pick up at the USO on Futenma that would take me to Foster, where I was soon playing basketball every day.

The organization surrounding Marine Corps basketball on Okinawa was impressive. There were tournaments and competitions through the year. There were staff NCOs and officers that reminded me of Coach Tex Williams in the way they organized leagues and tournaments and how they promoted them—taking out ads in the papers and such. There were teams all over the island and beyond, Okinawa to Andersen Air Force Base in Guam.

There were competitive leagues and teams recruited. Soon after I had arrived to Okinawa, I started playing on a team called Spotlight. The "owner" was the coach. He was a retired Marine that lived in Okinawa and owned a strip club. His wife was a retired stripper, and they had kids. It was a family that defied American cultural expectations, to be sure, but they seemed to be happy. After games, we always had a place to party.

We played in tournaments just about every weekend. There were always memorable moments. Once, flying to the island of Guam for a tournament, we found ourselves stuck without a place to sleep for the first night. We had flown over on a military transport plane. We got to Anderson late, and when we tried to check in at the barracks where we were supposed to stay, there was a problem. There were no rooms available until the next night.

Coach said, "Fuck it," and went to the commissary, picked up liter bottles of whiskey, rum, tequila, and a few gallons of water. We walked off base with the bottles and found a spot to camp out under a bridge. The bottles were already getting passed around before we sat down under the bridge for the night, somewhere on the island of Guam. We got drunk, bullshitted, laughed, and had a great time in that weird predicament.

The next day, we were scheduled to play first thing early in the morning. Coach tried to get our game time pushed back but the Airforce officials were not having it; we would play or forfeit the game. We could not believe our bad luck. Later, we learned from a friendly airman who went out drinking with us that our not having a room on the first night, and the early morning game the next day, was a planned conspiracy to get us off of our game. It was all an Airforce attempt to throw us off. We just laughed because it was a pretty good plot, and we would have done the same thing. Besides, the spontaneous party under the stars in Guam was the best part of the trip. To this day—though we did well in the tournament—that night drinking and joking with my fellow Marines under the open Guam night sky was my best memory of the trip.

And those tournaments were not the official ones. There were other tournaments that were sanctioned by the Marine Corps, played during the work day. These were base tournaments where you played with your command. Squadrons would put their best players against each other in tournaments, all in the name of boosting morale and seeing who would get the bragging rights. The standout players were pulled from their squadrons to play for the company. Company Commanders would have their teams to compete against each other. The level went to the first MAW all-star team, which played against the teams of the third Marine Division and the third FSSG (Field Service Support Group). I played for the first MAW and we won the tournament.

You have to be a good basketball player, but being good is not enough to be allowed to play. You have to have permission; your Company Commander and Sgt. Major must agree to allow you to play. In this respect, I was very lucky. My Squadron Commander not only gave me permission, he was excited to have one of his Marines on the team representing his squadron. When I played for the first MAW, the skipper and Sgt. Major would come to the games, and they would be proud to have me represent MTACS-18. The skipper would sign off on TDA (Temporary Duty Assignment) orders whenever I had the chance to play basketball, even if it meant my missing a deployment. I was very lucky to have a command so supportive.

After a few months on Okinawa, I was invited to try out for the All-Marine basketball team. Each year the Marine Corps invites thirty players—ten marines from the west coast (Pendleton and Miramar), ten marines from the east coast (Lejeune and Cherry Point), and ten marines from the far east (Okinawa: Hansen, Schwab, Futenma, Foster, etc.)—to try out for the All-Marine basketball team. The tryouts last a month but are over for a player as soon as he is cut from camp. My command approved my invitation and I was cut TDA orders to California, Camp Miramar, where the tryout camp would be this particular year 2005.

I was amazed at how strange life was and how you never know what can happen. Just seven or eight months ago, I was miserable, feeling down about my basketball days coming to an end.

I had felt hopeless, puzzled, and frustrated as to how my basketball career could come to what I felt was an unfair and disgraceful ending. Yet there I was, in the Marine Corps, getting paid to play the game I had dedicated my life to.

The tryouts were a lot of fun, but they were savage. There were no trainers or team of assents. It was only Coach Red and assistant, Coach Gunny Smith. Coach Red was a lifer (he was the type that would spend his life in the Marine Corps). He was formerly enlisted until he became a warrant officer, then he climbed the warrant officer ranks and turned captain, and when I met him for the All-Marine camp, he was a major.

On the first day of camp, he had the players get into groups according to the position we were trying out for. The point guards here, the shooting guards there, likewise the small forwards, power forwards, and centers. I could have played the one, two, or three positions, but I went to the small forward spot because players overloaded the one and two, four and five positions. Coach Red wrote what position we were going for beside our names on his roster. He said he'd be keeping twelve players.

The returning veterans were the captains and clearly had an advantage, something that Coach Red did not pretend to hide. But that did not mean their playing time was secure. When a returning vet was outplayed, Coach Red had the players flip jerseys. Playing time was based on merit. It was very competitive. All these guys had experience and some were very talented and athletic, many far more athletic than me. The play was rough. You did not drive into the paint without getting knocked to the floor. These players were grown men, and they were strong. Sometimes I was outplayed. But when you are moved off the starting team because you are outplayed, you understand, and the chance to win back the position is always there. All you have to do is step up.

We got straight to business. Basketball was our only job. The only military uniform we had to have was our alphas, and that was only case we got into some trouble and had to "stand before the man." We lived in a hotel just off base. There were two practice sessions a day. We were given rental vans for getting around (the returning vets on the team held the keys) and extra cash for food. "Rank" on the team was not according to your military rank, it was according to how many years you had played on the team. The highest status was for the players who were not only vets of the All-Marine team, but had played on the All-Armed Forces team. At the end of the All-Armed Forces Tournament, the coaches voted for twelve best players from the combined teams (Marines, Army, Airforce, Navy) to make up the USA All-Armed Forces team. This team would go on to play in the All-Armed Forces Tournament against the military basketball teams of the allied powers of Europe, in SHAPE (Supreme Headquarters Allied Powers Europe) Belgium.

I played the best basketball I had ever played. I was relaxed and playing my game. I could take in everything that was happening on the floor and comprehend in ways I never had before. The mental aspect of the game of basketball is so important, and I had been missing that. When you can relax your mind, your movements are far more fluid, reactions more precise. I was just playing and letting the hard work pay off, letting it happen, going with the flow. Sometimes I wished I could go back in time knowing what I had learned about the mental aspect of the game, the relaxing and having fun, the letting it happen. But not what I really thought about it. Did I want to go back to Mom crying? Have no money? The anger at the people hurting Mom? Having to move around? Waugh punting the basketball into the rafters? *No*. I had no desire to go back in time. My life had been a hard, ruthless, and vicious grind. It was happening now, so I would just go with it. Everything happens in its time. You just have to learn to go with the flow, have patience, and exist in the moment. You cannot always make sense of things. As Oliver Stone wrote in *Chasing the Light*, "sometimes a fighter cannot be logical; he just has to gut it out."

Camp lasted just over a month. Coach Red would cut two or three players at the end of each day. The players that were cut would have the following day to relax before flying back to their duty station. Coach Red was demanding but let the guys he cut have a day to drink up and enjoy California before sending them back. There was no doubt about my making the team; it was only a question of my placement in the rotation. I was having an excellent camp. It was as if all my basketball experience had been leading up to this moment. Finally, after all those years of hard work, it was paying off on the court.

By the end of the camp, coach had the twelve players he wanted to compete against the teams of other branches of the armed services in the All-Armed Forces Basketball Tournament. We had a slight disadvantage on the Marine team in that the Army, Airforce, and the Navy not only had larger numbers to select from, they all had more players with NCAA Division I experience. They had players out of West Point, Airforce Academy, and Naval Academy, all Division I NCAA programs. The Marine team was made up of players that were good, but I was the only college graduate with four years of Division I experience. But what I went through could hardly be considered a basketball experience, so I was more like them. For my other teammates on the Marine team, most of them had had an opportunity to play college ball, but life had somehow gotten in the way of their hoop dreams. Some had played a season of college, or junior college, but had to drop out because of trouble, or having to take care of a child, etc. In that respect, we all had something to prove.

I went on to play two consecutive seasons with the All-Marine basketball team. We finished second in the tournament behind the Airforce the first year, and second after the Navy the following year. After my second season with the All-Marine basketball team, I was selected for the All-Armed Forces team—out of the Army, Navy, Marine Corps, and Airforce—to represent the United States Military.

With the USA Armed Forces team, I played in Belgium at SHAPE in an international military basketball tournament. The US military went up against the best from the allied powers of Europe. And they really did bring their best. There players were not just from ranks of their military. Many of the other countries "enlisted" professional basketball players for the occasion. We still did well, placing third in the tournament. Even still, I was glad that we represented with players from our own ranks because it gave me the chance to play and end my basketball career on a positive note.

And this would, indeed, be the end. My hoop dreams been given closure. The All-Armed Forces team would be my last opportunity to play basketball full-time in the Marines. It was a kind of senior year, if you will. After the SHAPE international basketball tournament in Belgium, the USA All-Armed Forces team disbanded until the next season. I would never again play on All-Armed Forces team, or the All-Marine, because after my coming deployment, I would not be reenlisting. This time, my serious basketball playing days were really over, but this time it made sense and was with some closure.

Life truly is a mystery. It is hard to believe that I would get to experience vindication in this particular way. I could not have orchestrated such a thing if I tried. During the two years I was stationed in Okinawa, on Camp Futenma, I would, for the vast majority of the time, play basketball. I never once deployed with my squadron, which deployed to Thailand, South Korea, and the Philippines, while I got to play basketball. I will forever be grateful to my officers and staff NCOs at MTACS-18 for allowing me to play basketball for the Marine Corps. During my time on Okinawa, I played with Spotlight, the first MAW, the All-Marine basketball team, and the All-Armed Forces team. After that last season with the All-Armed Forces team, I flew back to Okinawa, to camp Futenma. My two-year orders to MTACS-18, Okinawa, were coming to an end and I would soon be rotating back stateside. I was receiving new orders. At my new duty station, there would not be time to play basketball.

Cherry Point, NC

I received orders to VMU-2 (Marine Unmanned Aerial Vehicle Squadron 2) in Cherry Point, NC. I considered myself lucky again because was staying with the Wing—the second MAW this time. The Wing culture was more my speed than the majority of the Marine Corps in that it was more laid-back. VMU-2 operated drones. The squadron's mission was to "provide aerial surveillance, offensive air support, and the electronic warfare for the II Marine Expeditionary Force." This squadron was directly involved in the Iraqi war and deployed every year.

I had not been performing my MOS—embarkation—because of all the basketball I had been playing, but I had still picked up rank because I had been keeping up with the basic Marine Corps responsibilities required for getting promoted. I was coming to my new squadron with the rank of Corporal—an NCO— and I was only a few months away from picking up sergeant. Promotion did not exclusively depend on performing your MOS. It is true that if you proved incapable of doing your job, it could hurt your chances for promotion. But that was not my situation. Whenever I was with my squadron, I quickly picked up the work at hand and fell in line. I also used the time I had while not playing basketball to keep up with the other responsibilities required for promotion that were not related to my MOS, such as MCIs, PFTs, and riffle range qualification.

The Marine Corps had a distance learning educational program. You send for an MCI (Marine Corps Institute) according to your rank and MOS and they send you the work to study and complete. There was basic coursework for all Marines, regardless of your MOS, and coursework specific to your job. I completed as many as I could, beyond the minimum, in order to get promoted more quickly. I would request the course, by mail or internet, and through the mail, I would receive a packet with textbook and accompanying test. I would learn the material well enough to complete the assessment, have it signed off by a superior, and mail it back. Upon successful competition, this accomplishment would be entered in my record, which increased my prospects for promotion to the next rank on the next promotion date.

PFTs (physical fitness test) had to be completed and entered into a Marine's record twice a year. It is a formal test, and if you did not get your score on the record, or you had a poor score, it would keep you from getting promoted. The test consisted of three events: sit-ups, pull-ups, and a three-mile run. To get a perfect score of 300, you had to do hundred crunches, twenty pull-ups, and an eighteen-minute three-mile run. All you needed for a first-class score was 235 points, which I always scored above. I never got a perfect 300, but I would get close. The better your score, the faster your chances for promotion, because you are scored against the Marines—in the entire Marine Corps—with your rank and MOS.

And, of course, there was the beloved rifle range. Twice a year, a Marine had to qualify on the rifle range, which was a week-long process similar to the format in recruit training. The minimum score was Marksman, next best was Sharpshooter, and the best was Expert. You still had to qualify in the firing positions of sitting, kneeling, and standing from 100- and 200-yard line, and in the prone position from 500 yards. Failure to keep up with this requirement would keep a Marine from getting promoted, and the higher your score, the faster your chances for promotion. So, I made sure to keep up with it and always shot Expert.

Making the All-Marine basketball team—or the All-Armed Forces team—did not matter as far as military promotion was concerned. It did not help or hurt. It helped with status and reputation but was not a variable in promotional algorithms between PFC and Sgt. I had to keep up with these other things if I was going to progress in rank. Basketball helped with making connections and an establishing respect with other Marines, but at the end of the day, the Marine Corps is in the business of war—not sports. When I arrived at VMU-2, I knew better than to try and use my basketball credentials as a prop to stand up on. I was not interested in doing that anyways. I did not define myself as a basketball player. Playing ball was now just something I did on the side. I did not need basketball anymore. I was my own man. I was ready to do my job and contribute my part to the mission.

In Iraq: With the Wing

After arriving to Cherry Point, I reported to the Sergeant Major of VMU-2 and was informed that I would be deploying to Iraq in less than three weeks. We would be deploying to the FOB (Forward Operating Base) Al Taqaddum (TQ), seventy-four kilometers west of Baghdad. It was a combat zone, but I was still going with the Wing, so comparatively speaking, I would hardly be ruffing it. Unless you are the type of Marine that is looking to get into a gun fight, life in the Wing is good. I had no desire for such thing. My enlisting was more about salvaging my broken identity than joining a good cause, or out of being patriotic.

I was thankful to be in the MAW, but I was still a little nervous about going to the theater, the war. But I would soon find out that the classification of "combat zone" for TQ was a bit of a stretch. The fighting was sometimes near, but it never came within the perimeters of TQ. And among all the Marines and Soldiers on TQ, the Marines of VMU-2 lived relatively well.

As far as the "tip of the spear" analogy goes, the MAWs were behind the grunts. It is the grunts of the Marine Corps that carry the weight of getting the kills, doing the dirty work. Grunt is a colloquialism for infantrymen: trigger pullers, door kickers, the pointy end of the spear, the guys who have to spend time in *the shit, the armpit, the crotch*. I cannot take credit for doing that kind of time in the war. I had access to hot showers and hot chow the entire time I was in country.

When a Marine gets orders to a MAW, it is often referred to as orders to "swing with the wing." Marines with noncombat MOSs were what grunts would sometimes call POGs (person-other-than-grunt). Some Marines resent being called that but I never minded it. After all, it was true. Most POG jobs are more relatable to civilian-like jobs than combat occupations such as machine gunner, artillery, or riflemen. I was a POG with orders to the Air Wing for the duration of my enlistment. During my time in Iraq, I never once had to pull the trigger on the enemy, or take fire. My MOS was support. By the time I arrived at VMU-2, I had spent six months in training and two years in Okinawa, where I mostly played basketball. I had been very lucky, and at VMU-2, my luck continued. The Marines there were good people. My Staff Sergeant, SSgt Benbow, showed me how to execute my responsibilities and clearly laid out the expectations. It was a smooth operation because this squadron had been deploying to Iraq every six months for the last three or four years. We had been alternating in country with VMU-1, stationed on the west coast air base Miramar, in California, for six months on, six months off rotation.

For me, an embarker, this was good news because it meant that the bulk of the equipment was already deployed and in place, the infrastructure already up and running. The facilities, the generators, the air conditioners, the motor pool, the flight line, the system of work orders, everything was already in place. I would be walking into an operation that had been in motion for years. The logistical work on my plate was the relatively small amount of gear and equipment that the various sections of squadron would be bringing.

The main element of my job was the preparing, packing, and staging of the gear to be deployed according to the means of transportation to be used. We would be moving almost everything by air on C-130s, so the boxes and containers we were taking had to be marked properly and staged on Air Force pallets, cargo netted securely, weighed, packing lists attached, and the load plans worked out and coordinated with the flight-line loadmaster. Embarkation specialist was a good MOS. It came with more autonomy than most, which I enjoyed and took advantage of. It gave me a slight portion of the kind of power that was not conferred by rank. Perhaps contraband could end up in a box or container that was not on the packing list? I was the guy to see. It was a job rife with underground connection, which I found exciting.

We flew over the Atlantic and stopped in Ireland for a refuel and a beer. I kept it Irish and had a Guinness and a Tullamore Dew. From there we went to Kuwait, where we would experience "death by PowerPoint" for three consecutive days. Finally, we loaded our magazines with live rounds, donned flak and Kevlar, and flew to TQ, hanging in the netted seats of a C-130. We arrived in the dead of night. Most of the Marines in our squadron had done this before, so I just went with the flow and pretended to know what I was doing.

By the time we completed the changeover with VMU-1, I had been promoted to sergeant and had a good understanding of what my job would entail while in Iraq. I would be managing and facilitating work orders and work requests from the various sections of our squadron, keeping up with the paperwork that ensured the steady delivery of fuel, and overseeing the delivery. Every week I would have to pick up the fuel from a staged location where an inconceivable amount of incoming supplies were flown and/or trucked in. I would ride shotgun for these pickups in a seven-ton truck. The gas came in ten-thousand-gallon rubber blivits, chained to an Air Force pallet. We would load them onto the bed of the truck with a fork lift, secure the load with cargo straps, and drive it back to our post.

SSgt Benbow had been on this deployment a few times. He never let me screw up. He would give me a hard time every once in a while, messing around, but when it came to business, he looked out and gave me credit for success that was really a result of his previous work. We had our own office. SSgt Benbow was the log chief. It was a makeshift, small building of plywood, framed with two-by-threes. SSgt Benbow and I each had our own desk, computer, and printer. Paperwork was part of our job. The motor pool was out back with the trucks, Humvees, generators, ACs, containers, etc. The building was wired up and powered by generators, so we had all the goods that come with electricity: AC, refrigerators, etc. The building was covered and draped in dessert camo netting, but it was generally understood that the enemy—Al-Qaeda and company—did not have the capability of attacking from the sky. There were no commercial planes to hijack out there, and our drones were in the sky 24/7.

SSgt Benbow kept things interesting. He kept a big jar of pickled pigs' feet on the outer corner of his desk. Because we were the point of contact for work requests and work orders, Marines had to come see us about getting things done. SSgt

Benbow had an unspoken rule that whoever touched the jar had to eat one of its contents. At least once a week, we would get a marine coming through, enquiring about a work order for something or other, and he would notice the big jar, stare at it, and invariably a conversation would start about the pickled pigs' feet.

"You like pigs' feet?" SSgt Benbow would ask and then say, "Go 'head an' pick it up. Have yourself a look."

And the Marine would pick up the big jar of pigs' feet and we would laugh and inform him of the rule.

"You'll have to eat one now, devil dog," SSgt would say in all seriousness.

SSgt never ran out of pickled pigs' feet, his wife back in the states was always sending them over. Every once in a while, he would scoop one out and make a show of eating it, as if it were the best food in the world.

Embarkation and logistics was the big business on TQ and a very interesting lens to look at the war through. The sheer amount equipment and supplies moving through this FOB was astounding. We had an internal network connection of correspondence around the base via phones, computer, and radio, with the FSSG, Division, the other MAW squadrons, and the KBR civilian contractors. TQ was like a wild west boomtown of the 1800s—a city that had sprung up in the desert. Things were being built. There were places to shop, order fast food, get a haircut, see a movie. The private contractors everywhere. KBR had their own swath of land on TQ where some of their employees lived in dumbfounding luxury.

There was not much ruffing it on TQ. Some of those KBR men lived like kings in their own duchy. My embark job often brought me in contact with some of these wild west bosses in the name of business. I would have to see someone about getting something or other: porta johns, exercise equipment, *you name it*. Sometimes they could not help but showoff and brag about how lavishly they were living. One KBR man showed me where he was living and invited me in. It reminded me of the trailer for the fictional character Jack Colt in the movie *Loaded Weapon 1*. On the outside, it was plywood, looking plain and nothing to speak of, but on the inside, it was a mansion with all the finery a modern life could offer. These guys loved to play the part of a cowboy in a spaghetti western. Most of them were big men with big beards and dark sunglasses, some actually wearing a holstered revolver on their waist, like Clint Eastwood or John Wayne.

The sounds of war were always in the distance— thanks to good work of the grunts—beyond TQ's perimeter. The grunts were always doing a kick-ass job, keeping the fight on the offensive, and then they would roll into TQ for some good food and rest, and then roll back outside the wire to pick another gunfight.

All the POG jobs in the Marine Corps are to support the Marine grunt. We don't use aircraft from the Air Force: our birds exist to provide exclusive support for the Marine commanders fighting the ground war. Marine Corps success, at the end of the day, is on the shoulders of the infantry. It was always big news and cause for celebration when one of the artillery units was able to use the intel that VMU-2 drones supplied to take out a target, or some of our infantrymen were able to rack up kill count, because of the intelligence that VMU-2 provided. That was the main point of our being there on TQ.

I was certainly no hero. All I did in Iraq was have a hand in the logistics behind the infrastructure that kept the drone/intel operation going. We all worked for the grunt. My part in the effort was relatively simple, and I did not have to endure any hardships. Once I took care of my responsibilities, I had leisure time on my hands. I could read, work out, or even play basketball. But I was beginning to develop a hunger for learning, so I was spending more and more of any leisure time I had reading.

Exactly how lights turn on in the mind will ever be a mystery to me. Out there in Iraq, I found myself interested in the *how* and *why* of things. The inner workings of the logistical machine on TQ was quite mind-blowing to me. The hands-on exposure seemed to wake me up to it. It made me realize—in a mind-altering way—that there was something going on in the world that I had not been paying attention to, or considering. I would see all the KBR contractors, the equipment, the supplies, the grunt convoys roll through, smoking their cigarettes, riding in vehicles riddled with bullets, exhausted, and it got me thinking: *What in God's name is going on?* There I was, in another land, another country, in a Middle Eastern desert, occupying and doing business. We were building structures and making roads. We had drones high in the sky, gathering intelligence for targets. C-130s, helicopters, and other types of "iron birds" were flying in and out at all times. Trucks were coming and going, delivering and picking up goods. There was a facility called "Hotel California," where the CIA was rumored to be keeping and interrogating high-level enemy combatants. The budget was unlimited. We named roads after American States. Out there, in the Iraqi desert, you could make a right on West Virginia and a left on Texas.

American KBR contractors and high-ranking military personnel were driving around in GMC SUVs, all of them toting pistols. There were "neighborhoods" with decked-out cargo containers as residences. TQ had its own fire department. We were bringing in businesses: McDonalds, AAFES, Commissary. There was a naval hospital. We had a banking system where you could sign for cash to spend. This was not just about grunts in gunfights; within the wire of TQ, we had created a commercial bonanza in the middle of a desert in the Middle East.

After months of all this sinking in, I began wondering what I had missed in school. Maybe I should have paid better attention. What was going on in the world? It was not just cancer and age killing people, men were killing each other. Governments were not just abstract ideas, they were people that directed armies and made life and death decisions on a colossal scale, with many people dedicating their life and work to enabling such a thing—myself included—to happen. I felt like I had no idea what I had gotten myself into. It was not as if the *Declaration of Independence* that was in Iraq—*we were*. And we had trucks, manpower, weapons, money, tanks, and tractors. We had cargo containers, cranes, and forklifts. We had generators, power cords, and air conditioners. We had lumber yards and motor pools. We had commissary, a postal exchange, and armories. We had contractors from the biggest companies in the world, from which you could get whatever you needed and much more. We had money to spend. We had SUVs, Gators, and four-wheelers. We had chow halls with steak and lobster and more types of ice cream than Baskin-Robbins. We had cases of Red Bull, dirty magazines, and if my KBR contact was to be believed, women from Third World countries ready for "marriage." It was astonishing, and I was amazed that many of my fellow Marines did not recognize the audacity. They carried on like such things were regular.

And perhaps it was *regular*. Perhaps it was me that had been living a naïve existence, chasing hoop dreams while there were far more serious things going on in a world from which I had been sheltered. My time on TQ was altering my perspective and changing my interests and priorities. I was becoming ambitious to educate myself. Maybe I should read those books that I had always ignored? I had gotten a taste in college, but the identity crises I was going through hindered my vision. Now that my vision had cleared up, this situation playing out in front of me in Iraq was quite something. Even the POGs carried weapons. From the Marines in the mailroom to Marines like myself, picking up products on a flight line or writing up a request for a forklift and a truck, we all kept an M-16 slung over the shoulder or a .9mm strapped to the leg, SAPI plates in our flak jackets, and four to six loaded magazines tucked into those flaks, ready to be inserted if some shit went down.

Even the civilian contractors had guns—all of them. Everybody was packing heat and the spirit of war was always in the air. It would have been suicide for the enemy to try something, which was why suicide bombing was their best weapon. They were dead anyways. We were so far ahead of the game that we had set down an FOB, that was in reality a full-fledged city, in the middle of the Iraqi dessert, with a massive supply depot where you could get anything you wanted. If the grunts were the hands and feet of the war machine, logistics and supply was the heart constantly pumping blood to those extremities. TQ was a supercenter of getting things and doling them out.

And there I was, in the midst of it all, now a Sergeant. I had made contacts. I was a guy who could get you a store-bought pint of whiskey, a case of Red Bull, or tobacco, straight from the truck. My S-4 officer made a Gator available to me to go on runs for various things. I would be speeding around from spot to spot—KBR campsites, flight lines, warehouses—taking care of business, greasing wheels, ensuring work orders were in progress, making sure we were getting the fuel for our vehicles and drones, that the porta-potties were getting serviced. And all of this madness had been going on years before I was dropped into the middle of it.

I was becoming interested in things. When I had leisure, my hands no longer reached for a basketball—they reached for a book. In what *things* I was interested, I could not say. Perhaps it was that I realized that I had been living my life completely blind to the bigger picture I now saw. I wanted to learn about it.

Thoughts on Moving Past the Game

If necessity is the mother of all invention, experience is the mother of all learning. You could sit through hundreds of lessons under the greatest of all teachers, but the lights of the mind will not illuminate until time and experience have given their blessing. As a coach is only as good as his players, a teacher is only as good as his students. I had been living with tunnel vision, and the light on the other end *had* to be the NBA or some other professional basketball playing option. It was a mirage of which I could not let go; my identity was wrapped up in hoop dreams. *I had to make it.* The push I had embraced to *make it* was, as Oliver Stone wrote so aptly in *Chasing the Light*, "I suppose really a race against myself in a hall of mirrors of my own making."

The Marine Corps became my rabbit hole—my way to escape unfulfilled dreams, frustrated ambitions, failure. My enlistment was a desperate grab for survival as I was in the midst of an identity crisis. And luckily, it worked out for my betterment. The Marine Corps was the "red pill" that showed me the matrix. Not that it was a cognizant, up-front choice like it was for Neo; I was stumbling through life, passing from day to day, not having much of a clue. But sometimes that is all you can do: keep stumbling through life, keep trying to get some footing. Finding that footing takes time.

The Marine Corps was not a random choice. Seeds had been planted since high school. I had come close to enlisting in high school and again toward the end of FUMA. But always just before I would give up on my hoop dreams, something would come along that would motivate me to keep going: Mom's cries, Coach Tex Williams pushing me, Coach Arritt, FUMA, the scholarship to Stetson University. *Maybe I could make it?* Just quitting the hoop dream trail, I would find another breadcrumb. *Maybe* . . . Without hoop dreams, I possibly would have dropped out of school. I most certainly would not have gone to college.

Not that I think everybody should go to college. No matter what you do in life, some form of "school" is taking place. You cannot avoid learning. You may avoid learning *some things*, but not *everything*. Sometimes you get choose one thing over another, and sometimes you do not even have a choice. The real "classroom" is not restricted to a room in a so-called school. Our world is our classroom. Learning is above and beyond any one individual, place, or moment. It is a combination of all things, the good, the bad, and—for all you Clint Eastwood fans—the ugly. When it all come out in the wash, the bad and ugly are as useful and important as the good in terms of getting you to where you need to be. All of life is conspiring to teach you as if God has made you his special project, and eventually, you have no choice but to listen. Cover your ears and try to block out the sound all you want, but what is going to happen is going to happen. Life has a way of continually turning up the volume. You have no choice *but* to learn.

In that sense of heightened understanding, Derrek Waugh was as important as any other coach I had along the way, perhaps more so. He was my final reality check before the Marines, perhaps what I needed to push me to enlist. Life is strange like that. In the classroom of life, Derrek Waugh was as important of an instrument as Coach Arritt. He was a terrible basketball coach, true enough, but what is basketball in the bigger picture of life? What does it matter? It was tough to go through, but the transformation of an identity usually is.

Basketball is a vehicle. To the immature young man, it will be his life because he is in the fog of his hoop dreams and does not have a strong enough sense of *self* to stand on his own, without the props that come with being a baller. The true significance of the game is in its role as a vehicle to help you get from where you are to where you are going. Basketball is never a final destination, no matter what level. It is never an end in itself. It is always a means to help you travel the path of your mystery, and everybody must eventually come to that understanding. It is as true for great NBA players as it was for me. In *The Breaks of the Game*, David Halberstam quotes former NBA player Jim Brewer, saying, "You think basketball is life but it's not. It's a front. You're isolated all those years you're playing ball. Shielded from everything, like living in a bubble . . . *it's* easy to get the idea that you're someone that you're not. Then one day it's over. The hard part is after the last game. That's when you need the attention the most and then suddenly it's not there . . . I sat around the house trying to figure out what went wrong, and waiting for someone to phone and give me another piece of my life."

We are often more desperate than we let on. We are trying to figure out who we are and how to express ourselves while not really knowing or thinking about our inner truth. We see ourselves not through our own eyes, but how we imagine we are perceived through the eyes of others. We unintentionally victimize ourselves through pressures of our own creation. Sadly, this is a lesson that every individual must learn on their own. Even a reader reading my words will not register these truths if he has not gone through a similar experience himself. His eyes will simply roll across these lines in passing.

Basketball, like so many other things, *can* be good in that it's a viable means of travel. It can help you develop as a man, give you something to do, and can be a kind of simulator to familiarize you with concepts of teamwork and working hard. But it is still just that—a simulator, a game. It can keep you occupied, travelling, moving, active, and engaged, but we all must eventually learn to define ourselves independently. Any destination outside of yourself is always a mirage, a metaphor, a way to deal that which is within. There is no such thing as "making it," because you are already there. The challenge is to realize it, to receive the gift of understanding.

My problem at Stetson was never Derrek Waugh; my problem was that I was looking to the game of basketball for inner fulfilment. That makes Derek Waugh—unwittingly—one of my greatest teachers. In a good story, the hero is only as strong as his villain. Our life is our story. While the people around us are continually being recast as we travel through time, we remain in our protagonist role, the hero. At Stetson, Derek Waugh was a villain cast perfectly in my life.

Our life is like a lie, a tale, a fiction. In the *Psalms,* it is written that "we spend our years as a tale that is told." Our truth is a lie to another man. Our perspective is just that—ours. An object up close is truthfully big and far away it is truthfully small, and if it is far enough away, it does not exist . . . *to us*. It all depends on where we are standing and the vision we possess. Therefore, we are the lie—our perspective, opinion—not the object.

Up until the Marines, I had been clinging to an identity that needed to die, because you cannot establish a new identity without killing off the former if it is so big that it will not allow for change. Derrek Waugh was the assassin I had to face. He was the man to successfully butcher the hoop dreams holding me back from ascending to my better self. He forced me to walk toward a better version of myself, all without either of us knowing it. In a Joseph Campbell *Hero's Journey* metaphorical way of perceiving life, there is indeed life after death. "Now that we're dead, my dear," sings Metallica, "we can live forever." Life is indeed a mystery in how the symbolism of baptism has such powerful range. The Apostle Paul wrote, "we glory in tribulations also: knowing that tribulation worketh patience; and patience, experience; and experience, hope . . ."

Like I said before, if necessity is the mother of all invention, experience is the mother of all learning. Good learning should give us hope. But how can you hope if you do not know who you are, what you are supposed to be? Developing an identity that suits you is challenging. Not even the most loving parent can help their children out in this department. The narrator in Lionel Shriver's *The Motion of the Body Through Space* says, "You could give your children opportunity, but you could not give them form—which meant that you could not give them what most children craved above all else. Were it possible to purchase for a daughter passion, intention, direction, and specificity—or whatever you called being-somebody-in-particular-ness—Serenata would have rushed off to the Identity Store before Valeria turned ten."

There is no such Identity Store. You can be fooled by shrewd merchants that associate a product with an image or dream, like LeBron sneakers and being a great basketball player, but that is the scam of marketing. Who you are as a basketball player is defined by what you do, not what sneakers you wear. So, naturally, I looked to the stats in the newspaper box score of my previous game to determine my value. During my last two years at Stetson University, in the box score beside my name, there was nothing there. I had no value.

Assessments have a place, but they must be kept in that place. To an extent, it is a noble thing to define your identity by your actions. "Faith without works is dead," wrote James. But context must be taken into account. There must be understanding, balance. The motive behind your actions is more important than the actions themselves. Aspiring to perform well in the game of basketball is in the spirit of healthy competition is acceptable. Aspiring to perform well in the game of basketball to define your value as a person, or to establish your identity, is to relinquish the power you have over assigning definition to yourself. In doing such a thing, you are forsaking your most preeminent power and right. This is why early success in life can become a trap. The major transitions in life are always the most difficult to face because they are situations where you have to make adjustments to how you have allowed yourself to be defined. It is almost a form of repentance.

The privilege to establish goals, and the decision as to what actions you will take, belongs solely to you and is only subject to your capacity and creativity. You will find that your capacity increased with the first step of realizing this truth. You really can create your own success. It is not hyperbole. "The least strained and most natural ways of the soul are the most beautiful; the best occupations are the least forced. Lord, what a favor wisdom does for those whose desires she adjusts to their power! There is no more useful knowledge," wrote Montaigne. I alone reserve all rights in deciding what goals I wish to peruse and may be as creative as I please in establishing how I go about fulfilment. Failure and success are a matter of the setup; it is all in the framing. It is not that there is no such thing as failure and success, winning and losing, but these things are concepts of the imagination, interpretation, and often artistically designed concoctions brought to life by wry, sharp, business-minded people that make money capitalizing on the dreams they sell us. They paint a picture and say *this is success, what it looks like, this is how you make it.* And because of our ignorance, lack of experience, self-confidence, and desire to *be somebody*, we buy it *hook, line, and sinker.*

Not only do we take up the role sold to us, *that we bought*, we look to others to define our value, ability, intelligence, to tell us whether we have succeeded or failed. As if another man or points on a scoreboard, or screaming fans, have the right to determine whether you *won* or *lost*. "There is no one but yourself who knows," wrote Montaigne, "whether you are cowardly and cruel, or loyal and devout. Others do not see you, they guess at you by uncertain conjectures; they see not so much your nature as your art. Therefore do not cling to their judgment; cling to your own." One of the favorite sayings of Socrates is said to be, "According to one's power."

Even enlisting in the Marine Corps was a desperate grab. I was still grasping for a new identity as per judgment outside of myself. The recruiting department of the Marine Corps had done their job. The image of *the few, the proud*, was stamped into my head. As if I needed the

Marine Corps for such a thing. I was no more patriotic, or nationalistic, than a dog. I had merely changed vehicles—from basketball to Marine—on my road of life. I was learning, but I had not learned yet.

A New Focus

Books have a unique and mysterious way of crystalizing our understanding. In Iraq, as my perspective began to shift again, I started reading books. I was not interested in going to school, I simply wanted to read. I did not want accolades, such as another degree or approval from a professor. I needed to exercise my mind in lecture and test my thoughts on paper. I would assess myself according to my goals and my judgement.

I read voraciously. The library in TQ was stocked with books: novels, classics, biographies, histories, you name it. There was a posted *Commandants Recommended Reading* list that recommended books according to rank. I took a look at the list and thought why not and started at the bottom with the recommended books for the rank of private and moved up the ranks: *Ender's Game* by Orson Scott Card, *Starship Troopers* by Robert A. Heinlein, *Rifleman Dodd* by C.S. Forester, *Fields of Fire* by James Webb, *The Last Stand of Fox Company* by Bob Drury and Tom Clavin, *With the Old Breed* by Eugene B. Sledge, *Marine Sniper: 93 Confirmed Kills* by Charles Henderson, *On War* by Carl von Clausewitz.

These were deep, philosophical books—especially the novels—to reflect and consider from that developed new platforms of perspective in my mind. I would get lost in these books for hours at a time. One book led to another and I would follow the leads as they presented themselves. Just like basketball players have a way of finding each other and playing, readers have a way of finding each other and talking about books, ideas. One reader I met gave me a short story he had written and asked me to read it and tell him what I thought about it. This encouraged me to push myself to write. It was the beginning of a different kind of education with a life of its own. It was learning for the sake of learning itself. Getting wisdom and understanding became a daily goal.

I had dabbled in writing from my time at FUMA, and my class work at Stetson, but this was different. This was like basketball when I played in the Marine Corps: no pressure, no particular assignment. I was reading and writing to challenge my thinking and see what I had to say. Writing is different from simply talking. It is more challenging. "If a man is commonplace in conversation and rare in writing," wrote Montaigne, "that means that his capacity is in the place from which he borrows it, and not in himself. A learned man is not learned in all matters; but the capable man is capable in all matters, even in ignorance." We will forever be ignorant of many things, but that does not mean that we cannot be capable, "even in ignorance."

Fictional literature is a most unique weapon—instrument of learning—in the service of education. Fiction is as important for illustrating truths, sometimes more so, than works of nonfiction. All stories, in a sense, are made up. Even if an author used "facts," he still assembles and shapes them into a plot according to his creativity. A good story, not data and facts, girds understanding. It is mysterious because our comprehension is heightened less by facts and data than the essence of a thing. If the storyteller cannot assemble the facts and data in a sexy, attractive way, who is going to internalize the message? Therefore, the fictional aspect, the storytelling, is where the truth is. Meaning is hardly ever on the surface. It is usually below, and you cannot take a look without jumping in.

Our life is as a tale. Even what was happening in TQ was a fiction. It was an idea that was made up and then brought to life. Think of building a house. An author creates the desired design. We call him the architect, but he is also an author. Therefore, building a house, writing a story, or going to war in Iraq, or writing a history: all start the same way in that they are an idea in someone's imagination. Then the steps to bring that vision to life are figured out and taken. Even in math we operate on a fictional platform. Mathematicians use numbers, but what are numbers? They are symbols representing something else, yet we use them without knowing what the numbers represent. We add in letters and call them variables. Everything that is happening around us is an exercise in creativity, fiction.

Reading, in my opinion, is nothing less than a portal into another dimension. That books are shaped in a rectangle, have a dull, boring appearance, and the words on the page are seen two-dimensionally, flat, word after word, line after line, is one of the world's greatest ironies. Despite the shape, there is nothing square about them. Reading remains the best kept secret in this world today, hidden out in the open, in plain sight.

It is not changing others, or the world outside of you, that is important. What is important to change is your thinking. Do that and the other stuff will fall into place. Good and evil are in the power of our perception, said Montaigne. True and false, fact and fiction; these are matters of context. Walter Mosley wrote that "truth . . . is just one man's explanation for what he thinks he understands." We might think we know something, but we are simply expressing our convictions.

Basketball became a nonfactor. I could take it or leave it. I will always be fond of basketball because it was the vehicle eventually leading me to books, but now I saw it in its context. Sometimes I would still play, but more often than not, I would rather keep reading the book I was on, or rework some ideas I had written. As my time was drawing a close in Iraq, I had a chance to reenlist in country and get a $30,000 tax-free bonus. For an enlisted Marine, that's a lot of money. But I did not reenlist. I felt like something was calling me to the outside, civilian world. I did not know what, but just like I knew when it was time to enlist, I knew it was time to separate from the Marines. And so, I did.

A Civilian Once Again

After I got back from Iraq, my four-year enlistment was soon up, and I separated from the Corps. I moved to New York, where I temporarily lived with a friend that was a former Marine, Chris Drews, now a cop for the NYPD, living in Yonkers. Mom was sharing an apartment on the Upper East Side of Manhattan with my sister, Jaime, at a place called Normandie Court.

Mom was still teaching for the DOE (Department of Education). She had been teaching special education at P.S. 108, a middle school in Harlem, ever since she moved to New York in 1998. Now it was 2007. Jaime worked part-time as an adjunct professor at the College of New Rochelle and Fordham University, Manhattan campus. She was working toward her PhD in social work. But Jaime was not doing well. She had a severe and debilitating case of multiple sclerosis that was getting worse by the day.

I started taking the steps to become an NYPD officer. I did not know what I wanted to do, so I would take whatever job came to me. Were it not for the 2008 economy crash, I might have been a cop. But the police academy, who had cycled only twice a year, did not have a class for a reason due to the financial crises. Mom was happy because she did not want me to be a cop; she wanted me to be a teacher. I was not averse to that. I did not necessarily want to be a cop either. I just needed a job. But to be a teacher, you had to get a master's degree, and I was not sure about the steps to start such a program. Mom was insistent. She took the initiative to sign me up for the standardized tests that were required to become a teacher, and when I paid her a visit, she gave me the information and told me where to go to take the tests, which I did and passed the two tests. They were annoying tests and it took the majority of my day. To this day, I do not know what those tests have to do with the job of teaching, or anything else. I suspect, like most standardized tests, they have something to do with money.

The fates turned up the dial. Jaime had an interview for an adjunct professor position at Mercy College in Dobbs Ferry. She needed a ride; I drove. As she was interviewing, I decided to walk around the campus, check out the gym, see what kind of basketball program Mercy had. As I was walking down a hall, I heard gospel music playing from an office. The door was opened, and there was a woman behind a desk, reading what appeared to be a Bible.

I had read the Bible a few times since I had gotten into reading, and I enjoyed talking with people about books we had read in common. I popped my head into the office and said, "That's a wild book. I've read it a few times."

"Hello," she said, "I'm Suzan. Can I help you with something?"

"Nah, I just taxied my sister here for a job interview. I was just walking around. I was going to check out the basketball court. Where's the gym?"

"You like the Bible?"

"Sure."

"You have a favorite part?

"Ecclesiastes."

"Definitely one of my favorites."

"Samuel as well. David's rise to power is fascinating stuff."

"Are you a teacher?"

"No. Why do you ask?"

"This is the office of education. The teaching program to become a certified teacher."

"Really?"

"Really."

"That's weird."

"Why's that?"

"I recently took the LAST and the ATSW. Mom's a teacher at P.S. 108. She thinks I should be a teacher."

"What do you do now?"

"Unemployed. I separated from the Marines a month or so back."

"You look like a Marine."

"Yeah. They did a number on me."

"Were you in Iraq or Afghanistan?"

"Iraq."

"Did you know that vets who served in Iraq or Afghanistan get 100% tuition paid, I believe? Have you spoken to our VA liaison?"

"No."

"Well, what's your name?"

"Joshua."

"Have a seat, Joshua."

Jaime did not get the job, but I was soon enrolled and matriculated into the education program at Mercy College, Bronx Campus. The Post-9/11 G.I. Bill paid the full tuition; I did not have to pay a dime. On top of that, I was given an E-5 BAH (Basic Allowance for Housing).

The fates turned up the dial again. I was regularly attending a store-front church in the Bronx, where my friend Chris Drews was attending with his family. To a church picnic, I gave a woman named Arigna Waters and her son, who was in the second grade at the time, a ride. The ride was about thirty minutes and Arigna talked the whole way, and as I listened to her, I got the feeling that this was *the one*. But I argued with myself as she talked, thinking that I was crazy. I didn't say anything, but I thought about her and kept an eye out for her for the duration of the picnic, and made sure nobody else gave her a ride back. She did a lot of talking on the way back as well, and as I listened, I could not escape the feeling that there was something between us. When I dropped her off at her apartment, I asked for her phone number, and she quickly gave it.

I told myself I would never get married, but I asked Arigna to marry me a week after asking for her phone number. She said yes. It was the summer of 2008. In the summer of 2009, our daughter Amy was born. At the time of this writing, 2021, We have been happily married since.

"Teach special education," said Mom. "You'll be able to get a job anywhere."

I matriculated into a program at Mercy College that would certify me for fifth to ninth grade as a "generalist" to teach students with disabilities. Mom was right about the need for special ed teachers. I got my first teaching job at I.S. 162, a middle school in the South Bronx, teaching a self-contained special education class. After an hour with my students, I understood why no teacher wanted the special ed job.

But it was not all that bad. I liked the kids. They were crazy as hell and that made things interesting. Overall, I saw it as a good job. I got weekends, holidays, July, and August. I was done by three every day. It did not bother me that my students were crazy as hell. I was crazy as hell myself. I felt like the curriculum and the state tests were bullshit anyways. I was as much a rebel teacher as they were rebel students. We were a good fit for each other.

The teaching job gave me time to continue my own studies, reading, and writing, which I was still vigorously pursuing. I changed schools a few times over the next few years, of my own volition, and found a good spot in District 79, at Passages Academy, Horizon, a juvenile detention center for 17-year-olds. At the time of this writing, I am still there. My students have inspired a good deal of writing out of me because it is hard to find the reading material that they will read. So, I write stuff they will like, laced with drugs, crime, and violence. I self-published a book on Amazon with many of these stories called *The Outer Streets: An Unconventional*

Urban Anthology under the pseudonym D. F. Wharton, along with a colleague, who contributed some writing and story ideas, under the pseudonym, T. Huffman.

Surviving and living well out here in the Bronx takes continual adjustments. You have to define the fight according to your favor, like Jack Britton did. *Fifty Grand,* a short story by Ernest Hemingway, shows how practical needs can cause a shift in one's ideological perspective, and how you have to adjust your definition of winning and losing according your needs. In the story—spoiler alert—the character Jack Britton ends up throwing the fight because he needs the money. He struggles morally with the decision, until the end, when he does what he has to do to get paid. He lost the fight by throwing it, but in reality, he won, because afterwards he was able to retire from boxing, a sport he was already too old to be doing. He did not have a pension or retirement plan. In the story, you see from the perspective of Britton, and it challenges your own opinion on the situation. It was a situation where the *wrong* thing was actually the *right* thing for Jack.

It is important to read to push your perspective around and see things through different eyes. Reading is a simple way to get outside of yourself. So, I push myself to read every day, even if I am tired. I draw from the way I learned to work hard in basketball, and push myself through the pain, which is a characteristic that has stayed with me and helps me push myself as a student, a teacher, a reader, and a writer.

The biggest lesson to learn is how to face and come back from failure, to find the strength to make an identity change. It is a universal problem for adolescents, but among gangbangers and the incarcerated population, the identity trap seems especially vicious. Many of them embrace a thug life, drug-dealing, gun-toting gangster image, and they become stuck in a continual cycle of having to "prove" themselves to everybody around them. It is a way of thinking that makes prison the "NBA" for criminals, and by the time many of these young men realize how insane the cycle is, it is too late. With some of them, maintaining their self-image is a twenty-four hours a day job, and they keep getting themselves incarcerated—without thinking about it—for the sake of maintaining an image. I think our self-image can become more confining than an actual prison. Think about that.

A lot of politicians and educators talk about poverty, race, and social injustice, but they do it in a way that does not help and is more antagonizing than anything else. I think these kids need to keep hearing and reading good stories, not have all the disadvantaged poverty talk drummed into their head. It makes it too easy to play the victim instead of just changing their self-image and behavior. Writers like Walter Mosely, S. A. Cosby, George Pelecanos, and

Stephen King are doing a better job of teaching than actual teachers.

I try to take the things I get from these writers into my classroom. The biggest goal of education, I believe, should be engagement and trying to help students to make adjustment with respect to their perspective. The standardized tests do not help. Maybe those tests could have a place in more exclusive areas of study, but to force the general student population—who are for the most part just trying to figure out who they are, and who they want to be—to take the test and then define their intelligence based on what they do not know is a mistake.

My students, like everybody else, are going through an identity crisis. They would be better off watching good movies and reading good books, and they are simply encouraged to reflect on a character they can relate to. If students are struggling readers, it should not be beneath the teacher to use more movies. Put on the subtitles.

Encourage reading as much as possible but do not make a student's weakness the sole focus. You have to make *possible* goals so the student can experience success. This "high expectation" mumbo jumbo is a bunch of foolishness. Even great three-point shooters warm up close to the basket.

Many parents and educators need to come down off their ideological high ground about state-sponsored rigorous curriculums that do not do kids much good, and this has nothing to do with the economic situation at home. Montaigne wrote of his early education that his teachers would "teach me to enjoy knowledge and duty by my own free will and desire, and to educate my mind in all gentleness and freedom, without rigor and constraint."

Not that I pretend to have all the answers. Every situation calls for a different set of actions and activities. You cannot be wedded to a lesson plan as a special ed teach. You have to be loose and flexible, able to go with the flow. There is no *one way* to teach and learn. Kids need room to figure out who they want to be. Everybody gets it wrong at first. Chuck Palahniuk wrote somewhere in his book *Consider This* that people do not start to figure out who they are until around thirty and then have to start over.

I will always be partial to sports, and I wish they were more important to the people who make decisions in the DOE. I did not become interested in academics until years after college. Sports were pretty much the only thing that I responded well to in school. And through sports, I learned things that would help me academically: how to work hard, push myself, struggle with fatigue, meet resistance, and then go a little further. Metaphorically, Dad was teaching me how to finish a writing project with our basketball workout. I did not like school back then, when I was working out with Dad. I never did any reading or writing. My illusions, my hoop dreams, kept me focused.

So as a teacher, I do not try to force academics in the "rigorous" fashion of the times. I already know it cannot be done; learning will happen in its own time and is not something you can force. Stressing out over test scores and setting about to create a "sense of urgency" in the classroom is a game I know better than to start. Doing such a thing would only complicate my relationship with the students, and relationship is everything. In *The Motion of the Body Through Space*, Lionel Shriver's narrator says "no gambit better assured victory in any game than refusing to play it in the first place." Right on, Lionel. Life and experience are the only real teachers out there. I do more talking than teaching. We are all students. Every once in a while, there are "teachable moments," but I am no more in control of them than I am anything else. All that any of us can do is keep pushing ourselves in the work we have found for ourselves. People, other than yourself, are going to be who they are; you have to concentrate on being you. It is foolish for a so-called teacher to think he is in control of the change within another human, especially when the teacher struggles to make changes within herself. "Natural inclinations gain assistance and strength from education;" wrote Montaigne, "but they are scarcely to be changed and overcome." Learning is a mystery certainly not exclusive to compulsory education. If the idealists knew how to manufacture it and make it happen, then life would not be the way it is.

As it stands, we do not know how to grow an ambition for genuine learning in the heart of man. All we can do is be thankful for what we have and do our best. Solomon wrote, "Whatsoever thy hand findeth to do, do it with thy might; for there is no work, nor device, nor knowledge, nor wisdom, in the grave, whither thou goest." Basketball was the first thing my hands found to do, and I worked on my game with all my might. It did not take me to where I thought it would, or where I wanted to go, but it took me somewhere better: right here, thinking, writing, still working hard, still pushing myself, and I have adjusted my perspective and taken charge of the game I am playing, and I have rigged it to my advantage: *no gambit better assured victory in any game than the refusal to play it in the first place.*

Made in the USA
Middletown, DE
24 March 2022